BALLS

HOW TRUMP, YOUNG MEN, AND SPORTS SAVED AMERICA

CLAY TRAVIS

CENTER
STREET

NASHVILLE–NEW YORK

Center Street
Hachette Book Group
1290 Avenue of the Americas, New York, NY 10104
centerstreet.com
@CenterStreet/@CenterStreetBooks

First Edition: November 2025

Center Street is a division of Hachette Book Group, Inc. The Center Street name and logo are registered trademarks of Hachette Book Group, Inc.

The publisher is not responsible for websites (or their content) that are not owned by the publisher.

The Hachette Speakers Bureau provides a wide range of authors for speaking events. To find out more, go to hachettespeakersbureau.com or email HachetteSpeakers@hbgusa.com.

Center Street books may be purchased in bulk for business, educational, or promotional use. For information, please contact your local bookseller or the Hachette Book Group Special Markets Department at special.markets@hbgusa.com.

Library of Congress Control Number: 2025942958

ISBNs: 9780316598934 (hardcover), 9780316598958 (ebook)

Printed in the United States of America

LSC-C

Printing 1, 2025

TO PAPA LARRY KORNACKI, WITHOUT
WHOM OUTKICK WOULD HAVE
NEVER EXISTED.

CONTENTS

O
N MARCH 17, 2022, Lia Thomas, a 6-foot-3, 210-pound swimmer with long arms and legs stood on the starting blocks of an Atlanta, Georgia, pool. It was the women's NCAA championship, a culmination of the college swimming season, the 500-meter freestyle finals.

Cheering spectators packed the stands.

As eight swimmers prepared to dive into the water, broadcasters analyzed the field. "Expect for Lia Thomas to go out fast," one commentator said on the ESPN+ broadcast, "just like she did in the preliminaries."

There was no mention of one very important reason why Lia Thomas might be expected to go out fast in a field of women's swimmers: Lia was a man, born Will Thomas, a former male swimmer for three years on the University of Pennsylvania men's team who had decided he was female. Now Will, renamed Lia, who had been a below average male collegiate swimmer, was poised to become the best women's collegiate swimmer in the country.

The starting buzzer sounded, and all the competitors dove into the pool.

A 500-meter race is a long one, requiring twenty laps in the pool and phenomenal physical stamina. On the initial leap, Lia Thomas soared past his female competitors, and as the laps added up, he increased his lead over the other best college swimmers in the country. The ESPN announcers described the scene down the final stretch of the race this way: "Lia Thomas pulling away over the final 150 meters, had to work for it, she was pushed over the first 350 meters."

Then as Thomas touched the wall long before his competitors, ESPN concluded, "Thomas wins the NCAA championship . . . and it was those final 100 yards where Lia Thomas really pulled away."

"Yes, that's when she really took control of the race," intoned the other analyst.

She.

Over and over again, Thomas, who until recently had been competing as a man in men's swimming for the University of Pennsylvania, was being referred to as she by the male broadcasters working for ESPN.

At no point during the race was the fact that Thomas was a man, swimming with a penis, in a women's bathing suit, in a pool full of women, addressed in any way.

The ESPN announcers continued their analysis: "Emma Weyant did as much as she could to hang in there and did a spectacular job getting second. She went her best time by two plus seconds . . . and Thomas swims a personal best this season as well . . . to win by nearly two seconds."

A win by nearly two seconds!

That's an extraordinary margin in swimming.

In a sport where winners are often determined by fractions of a second, where we've all seen super slow-motion close-ups to determine whose hand hit the wall first, Lia Thomas won an NCAA championship by nearly two full seconds.

And Emma Weyant, the woman who came in second, wasn't just any swimmer herself; she won a silver medal in the 400-meter individual medley in 2020, and four years later, at the 2024 Olympics, she would win the bronze. Emma Weyant was an Olympic-level standout swimmer, one of the best women's swimmers in the world.

Yet Lia Thomas had just beaten her by nearly two seconds in a race featuring the best women's swimmers in the country.

Only in the postrace ESPN interview was Thomas's sex alluded to in any way, but only as a "controversy" that Thomas needed to overcome.

A viewer who didn't know any better wouldn't have understood what had just occurred: a male swimmer, identifying as a woman, had just been crowned the greatest women's swimmer of the collegiate women's swimming competition in the 500-meter freestyle race. A man was officially a women's NCAA champion in the record books.

Back home in Nashville, I watched the competition and wrote a tweet: "Lia Thomas wins women's 500 meter NCAA swimming competition, celebrates by twirling penis like a helicopter."

It was a banger of a tweet, one that would have echoed across the Twitter universe, with equal measure cheers and jeers.

One that, unbelievably, no one else in all of sports media could send without getting canceled.

Honestly, I loved it.

Because it perfectly distilled, with humor, the absurdity of the sports competition we'd all just watched.

But I deleted it and didn't push send.

Why?

Because OutKick, a sports website I'd founded in 2011, was covering the Lia Thomas story in a profoundly serious and fair manner, and I didn't want to distract from the hard work so many of our writers were doing on this story. For once in my life, I actually didn't draw attention to myself. I did my best to behave like an actual adult.

But as I sat contemplating the ridiculous absurdity of where we were in sports—a man had just won a women's sports championship by claiming he was a woman, and most in sports media were treating it as normal, courageous, and brave—I couldn't help but think, *How in the world have we gotten here?*

A few months later, ESPN, the nation's largest sports company, aired an ad celebrating Lia Thomas as one of the top women's athletes of the year.

The full one-minute honorarium said Thomas was a hero for becoming the first trans woman to win an NCAA Division One championship.

Thomas himself, according to the *Washington Examiner*, even began to compare himself to Jackie Robinson. Robinson, of course, was the first black Major League Baseball player. Now that the woke mind virus had taken over at ESPN, and all of the rest of sports media too, a man was being praised as one of the best women's athletes of the year.

I felt like I was taking crazy pills.

How was it possible that OutKick, my sports site, and our employees were the only sports media company that would attack this absurdity in any way? How had everyone else in sports lost their minds?

Indeed, the beginnings of the Lia Thomas story had emerged on our website when a women's swimmer on the University of Pennsylvania team sent a Twitter direct message to one of our writers to alert him to what was taking place. Did we know, she asked, that a man was identifying as a woman and setting records in women's swimming?

The women's swimmer requested full anonymity to tell her story because she was terrified of what would happen to her if she used her own name. And she was messaging OutKick because she knew we were the only sports site on the internet that would even cover her story.

Back in March of 2022, I didn't know it yet, but that direct message on Twitter, which I will explore in detail later, was the first ripple of what would become a massive tidal wave, a red tsunami that would sweep Donald Trump to a colossal win in the 2024 election.

Remarkably, the tides have shifted in women's athletics to such a degree that in July of 2025, the University of Pennsylvania even agreed to remove all of Lia Thomas's records from the Penn athletic records and apologize to Thomas's former teammates for allowing this to happen. OutKick's victory on this issue just continues to grow thanks to the political tides shifting.

This book will explain how Trump used sports, particularly through the prism of male voters, to win the biggest landslide election for a Republican presidential candidate since 1988. In the process, Trump didn't just win the election; he moved all fifty states redder, from New York to California, Florida to Washington, and all points in between.

How did he do it?

When it got right down to it, Trump had balls.

And the Democrats didn't.

But before 2024 could happen—heck, before a man could win a women's NCAA championship in 2022—woke sports had to first take over.

How did that happen? How did we go from sports being a unifying connective tissue for fans of all different backgrounds to it becoming the vanguard of left-wing identity politics? It all started on July 15, 2015, when Caitlyn Jenner received an ESPY for bravery on ESPN's primetime broadcast, simulcast on ABC.

That was the moment when, for the first time, woke sports took over the American sports universe. Before we can understand how Donald Trump won in 2024, we first have to figure out how Lia Thomas came to be standing on the medal stand as the first man to win an NCAA women's swimming championship.

Lia's win didn't happen in a vacuum. It was all part of the process of woke culture taking over sports. And that began to happen in 2015, with Caitlyn Jenner's ESPY for courage.

CHAPTER 1

Before Sports Went Crazy

SOME OF YOU READING THIS BOOK are going to know who I am, but, staggeringly to me, some of you are going to be reading this book and have no idea who I am or what I do. Seriously, what have you been doing for the past twenty years of your life?

Do you even get on the internet?

We all know how this book ends. Donald Trump is elected president in a landslide victory thanks to the union of young men and sports fans. Sometimes you can judge a book by its cover. But most people still don't understand how that happened, how Trump moved all fifty states in his direction, how he won the most impressive Republican electoral victory since George Bush Sr. in 1988. The truth is it didn't happen overnight. First, the woke virus had to infect sports and then the culture had to swing back against far-left excess. My always humble opinion, as you've seen from the Introduction, is that the Lia Thomas women's sports victory crystallized for many people that things were moving in the wrong direction. But in order to understand how that moment came to be, you need a quick roadmap of the descent of sports from meritocracy, the best man *or* woman wins, to madness, the best man pretending to be a woman wins. How did this happen? Well, thankfully, I had a front-row seat for the path from meritocracy to madness.

And here's a quick background through my own story: In 2004, as a recent graduate of Vanderbilt Law School, I got married and moved to the US Virgin Islands, where I started work at the biggest law firm in the Caribbean, which had thirteen attorneys. While working as a lawyer, I had a quarter-life crisis and began to write and post articles online with friends of mine.

I started writing online, legitimately, with an audience of zero.

That site we started with friends grew in popularity, and in the fall of 2005, I started to write online sports columns for CBSSports.com, which published my columns for free on their site. In 2006 I wrote my first book, *Dixieland Delight*, which was published a year later. It was the story of my traveling to all twelve SEC football stadiums in the same year. (This was before the SEC expanded to add fourteen and then sixteen teams). The book was a zany, irreverent, fun travelogue that sought to examine why SEC football had such a deep connection to the culture of the South.

Then came another book about SEC football, *On Rocky Top*, a story of the 2008 Tennessee Volunteer football season told from the perspective of a lifelong fan who is given unlimited access to his favorite football team. My Volunteers went 5–7, their head coach Philip Fulmer was fired, and my book came out in 2009.

The same year I wrote *On Rocky Top*, I moved from writing at CBS to Deadspin, then the most popular sports blog on the internet. I was making a good living, but as an associate editor, I didn't get along with the managing editor, A. J. Daulerio, who would eventually be promoted to run Gawker.com, a position from which he would bankrupt the entire company by posting a clip from a sex tape of Hulk Hogan. But that was a few years in the future. Back then, at the end of 2008, I left Deadspin and eventually found a job writing at FanHouse.com, which was the sports front page for AOL.com. (In those days many people still began their internet visits on AOL.com, so the audience for articles that were posted on the front page could be extraordinarily large.)

At thirty years old, after five years of full-time work, I was making $25,000 to write about sports on the internet. But after a couple of years of diehard work for FanHouse.com, I'd been promoted to national columnist at the site, my salary had been bumped up to $40,000 a year, and a long-awaited raise was on my boss's desk. When it was signed, I would be making six figures to write my opinions about sports.

With two young kids, a son born in 2008 and another son born in the fall of 2010, I legitimately didn't believe my life could be any better.

And it wasn't just writing about sports. Thanks to the fact I would take any invite to be a guest on sports talk radio shows, I had discovered I was a pretty good radio guest too. Being a radio guest led to a radio job. So in the spring of 2008, I had begun a Tuesday-night radio show on 104.5 the Zone in Nashville, Tennessee. When we weren't preempted by Nashville Predators hockey games, my friend Chad Withrow and I would do two hours of radio from seven to nine one night a week.

Initially we were unpaid for the radio show.

After about six months, I got my first paycheck for radio. The two of us split $100, $50 each, sponsored by Otter's Chicken Tenders, a local restaurant near Music Row on Nashville's Demonbreun Street. We had sold the ad ourselves, and this advertisement would become the first of many that I would personally sell to fund my media endeavors.

That one-day-a-week show eventually led to an opportunity to be part of a three-man show from noon to three, central. We called it "Three Hour Lunch," and I was paid $45,000 a year for that job.

So by January of 2011, I had two sports media jobs, clawed my way up to an $85,000 yearly income, and felt like I could take care of my young family.

As 2011 started, my wife and I had two young kids at home, ages three and four months, and things were going so well that our hope was she might be able to quit her job as a high school guidance counselor and stay home with the boys all day instead of needing to work.

Then, as so often happens, the bottom fell out of our life.

In early January of 2011, I got fired along with everyone else working at FanHouse.com.

Our company had been acquired by SportingNews.com, and just like that, my big extension, my promised six-figure job, was gone.

After seven years of grinding to build a writing career in sports media, I had almost nothing to show for it. I was a thirty-two-year-old father of two when this happened, and suddenly I faced a real challenge in my own life: What would I do to take care of my family? After seven years of full-time grinding to make a living in sports media, I had a midday radio show paying me $45,000 a year, and the job I loved—writing about sports—suddenly didn't exist at all.

Some of you reading this have likely found yourself in similar situations in your own careers. I really didn't know what to do. There were many nights where I would lie awake and wonder if I should give up on my dream of working in media and just go back to practicing law full-time to take care of my young family.

Thankfully, my stepfather-in-law, Larry Kornacki, who had run his own business for most of his life, saw something in me. Over many conversations, he encouraged me to start my own sports site. Ultimately, without his prodding, I'm not sure I would have taken the step at that point in my life, but I just kept coming back to one question: Did I really want anyone else to control, ever again, my family's own financial future?

Two things happened that helped to convince me to launch my own site.

First, I'd learned the radio advertising business. One day that year I'd been out on ad sales calls—I encourage all "talent" to do ad sales calls; it's how you actually get paid—with a hair-replacement advertiser. Sports talk radio, which targets men ages 25–54, makes the majority of its ad money from dick pills, hair replacement, mortgages, sports gambling, and cars. I did live-read ads convincing bald men to get hair replacement. A "live read" is the one you hear a radio guy do as he goes to commercial break. Generally speaking, these are the most expensive ads in radio because the host is ad-libbing, which generally lasts around a minute, and is providing a direct, personal endorsement of a company or product. I was paid $50 for every live read I did on the radio show, and we had only nine of them to sell for every show.

That summer, my jaw dropped when I saw the company stroke a check for $50,000 for me to do live reads for their hair-replacement company. Here was one advertiser paying more for live reads from me than I was set to make in an entire year of radio shows. And he was doing it because I was so good at getting people to buy hair.

It was eye opening because I realized I was busting my ass to make pennies on the dollar. Given that social media was exploding in popularity, I could see that the future was with individual talent, not with large, preexisting platforms. It felt obvious to me. Social media was going to be far more about the name on the back of the jersey than the name on the front.

If individuals were going to rise in influence and significance, why should I beg to work for a big company again when that big company would be able to fire me, like what had just happened at FanHouse.com, even if I was doing great work?

Second, around May of that same year, I vividly remember attending a local Nashville Sounds minor league baseball game. The Sounds were a Triple A team, the last stop in the minor leagues before Major League Baseball. I remember sitting in the stands that day, watching the game and thinking that I was the equivalent of a Triple A player in my career. For the past seven years, I'd worked tirelessly to try to make a career in sports media, and I'd gotten achingly close to breaking into the big leagues.

I'd written a couple of best-selling sports books. I'd become a national columnist. I was cohosting a sports talk radio show in my hometown. But almost my entire salary on radio went to paying for day care. I had a mortgage to pay, kids to help raise and take care of, and a wife who didn't particularly like her job, because it took her away from our kids and didn't pay well either. What if this was just where I was going to end up, a Triple A talent, someone who got close to the big leagues but never was able to push through and play at the highest level?

That night I went home and lay awake in bed for a long time thinking about what the right choice was. Ultimately, I made a decision: For better or worse, I wanted to control my future, to succeed or fail based entirely on my own choices in sports media.

In 2011 in a Birmingham, Alabama, hotel room I was staying in for Southeastern Conference Media Days, I clicked publish on the very first article on a brand-new website I'd founded, OutKicktheCoverage.com.

That day's articles mostly focused on the biggest news from SEC Media Days: the continuing scandal surrounding whether Cam Newton, the Heisman trophy–winning star quarterback for the national champion Auburn football team, had been paid to play for the Tigers, thereby violating NCAA amateurism rules. It sounds quaint in today's modern Name, Image, and Likeness era, but players weren't allowed to be compensated in any way to play college sports back in 2011, when I launched the site.

I wrote all the articles, sold all the ads, legit did everything for several years all by myself. As you might imagine, like many people who founded a small business, I worked all the time. Virtually all of my waking hours were spent on the site.

While I was working all the time, I had good luck with my timing. In the summer of 2011, shortly after I launched the site, expansion fever took over college football. The SEC, Big Ten, Big 12, and the Pac 12 were all looking to expand. Eventually Texas A&M and Missouri would join the SEC; Maryland and Rutgers would join the Big Ten; Colorado and Utah would join the Pac 12; and West Virginia and TCU would move to the Big 12.

If you loved everything about college football, like I loved everything about college football, you probably found conference realignment exhilarating. I loved that realignment required analysis of sports, business, politics, and the law because all four factors played substantial roles in the ultimate outcome. OutKick broke a series of major stories in those days about realignment, and our audience began to grow. (Not everyone agreed with my obsession on this story. My wife pronounced college football realignment, "The most boring story in the history of sports." And her opinion didn't get better when we took our first vacation without our two boys, a three-day getaway to Las Vegas in August of 2011. The moment we went to the pool news broke on Twitter that Texas A&M was joining the SEC, at which point I told her I had to go back to the room and work. To her credit, she didn't complain about me needing to work on our vacation.)

This was, by the way, the first time I ever met my friend Todd Fuhrman, who was working in the sports book at Caesar's. We met because Todd slid into my DM's saying he'd loved *Dixieland Delight*. The first time I met him was in the Caesar's sports book. I brought him an autographed copy of the book, which he has made fun of for years. But who wouldn't want an autographed copy of my book? How many better gifts are there?

Back in 2011, I was hoping to get a gambling company on as an OutKick site sponsor, and my goal on the trip had been to meet Caesar's executives and convince them to buy ads. (Remember that I was selling all the ads on the site too.) I felt like sports gambling would eventually get legalized, and when it did, it would transform all of sports media. I was right, but that was still seven years in the future. Todd and I would later go on to work together doing TV for nearly a decade, including the first-ever live show from a Las Vegas casino on Fox Sports 1 in the spring of 2014, but that was still years in the future too.

In the meantime, I covered conference expansion obsessively, but we also had lots of fun on the site. My goal was to publish at least one long article a day with several shorter ones. Along the way

I followed our site traffic zealously on Google Analytics, leaving it up on a laptop screen all the time so I could see what people actually read, not what they claimed to be interested in reading. I was always learning from what the data showed me, and I'd adjust my articles accordingly. I've never understood why anyone working in any business wouldn't want to use the data to make them better at what they did for a living.

Yes, conference realignment, which dealt with the complexities of sports, business, and politics, could be a major draw but so could fun, zany stories about college life. For instance, in 2012 Johnny Manziel, the freshman quarterback at Texas A&M, went out for Halloween dressed as Scooby Doo and found himself dancing next to a girl dressed in skimpy black lingerie and another wearing a pink Playboy-bunny outfit. The shot that went mega viral, and I still believe helped to make him an internet superstar, was Manziel in the full Scooby Doo costume grinding on a hot blond in black lingerie, a black bikini top, black panties, knee-high socks, garter belts, and heels.

A reader sent me the photos, and the minute I published them online, the site almost melted down.

As major scoops go, this wasn't Watergate.

But a few weeks after that Halloween performance, Manziel went on the road and beat Alabama, propelling him on a rocket ship to stardom and the Heisman trophy too. Manziel, following on the heels of Tim Tebow and Cam Newton, helped to make the SEC the center of college football, and OutKick had become the foremost independent site for SEC fans to entertain themselves online.

My audience of mostly younger college football fans, men in particular, loved looking at stories like these, and, frankly, no one else would cover stories like them. I had a monopoly on Manziel and hot girls, and it turned out college football fans liked Manziel and hot girls.

We also featured a regular collection of drinking games to print out and play along during big college football games, typically located in the Southeastern Conference. The South became our solid base of readership, and we started to rack up hundreds of thousands of readers, mostly younger guys around my age who were looking to be entertained at work.

In addition to my success with OutKick, on the radio front, we'd moved to drive time—a new 3–6 P.M. daily window—and I'd negotiated big salary increases for my cohosts, Brent Dougherty and Blaine Bishop, and me because I knew how much money the station was making off us. The station offered us a small raise, and I said it wasn't enough. We all wanted to triple our salaries, and we wanted to remove the clause in our contracts that allowed us to be fired at will and replace it with for-cause termination. (Even to this day, most radio contracts aren't worth the paper they are printed on. My "contract" allowed me to be terminated at any point in time with no severance, and I had a six-month noncompete if the company fired me. Given that most radio talent doesn't make that much money, a six-month noncompete was impossible for most of us to ever serve out and remain in radio. Essentially the radio companies, Cumulus, at the time, had us by the balls. They could fire us at any moment, and they could prevent us from working for half a year. How many people reading this could survive six months with no income in their current industry? Back then, there was no way I could have. Cumulus is not my favorite radio company, by the way. In 2014, I quit radio with 104.5 the Zone after the company offered me a $5,000 a year raise. That equated to $20 a day; I could have gotten a side job at McDonald's and made more. Rather than counter their offer, I told them I was quitting. By 2020, with my OutKick company well established, in order to hire a new behind-the-scenes employee, Cumulus insisted we pay them a $5,000 buy-out. Otherwise they were going to cancel my colleague's wife's health insurance. Oh, and she had brain cancer. Yeah, this is radio.)

Thanks to my aggressive negotiation, the station tripled my salary, and ad dollars were rolling in on OutKick so that I was making over $100k there too. In the space of a few months, I'd gone from making $45k a year and questioning whether I belonged in sports media at all to making over $250k a year in radio and writing.

Things were going so well that by the summer of 2011 my wife quit her job as a school guidance counselor, allowing her to stay at home with the boys, and things just kept getting better from there.

By 2013, just two years after OutKick was founded, I was making a good living on OutKick and radio. Fox Sports, which was launching its new broadcast network, FS1, came calling. They licensed my site's content and brought me over to appear on their college football pregame show, hosted by Erin Andrews, a former Florida Gator grad who had become a fan of OutKick and suggested me as a hire to Fox.

Fox gave me a three-year, $1.2 million contract and took over ad sales for OutKick while allowing me to retain ownership of the site. This way all I had to do was write on the site, not sell ads too. Combining that deal with my local radio show, I was suddenly making over $500k a year.

From thinking I was going to have to quit sports media to all of this in the space of just two years, I truly felt that everything was perfect.

That fall, in 2013, I was on a college football pregame show for Fox Sports—traveling to Los Angeles every weekend—and I was making plenty of money to pay off my mortgage and raise my family without any financial worries.

Sports was, up to that point, almost entirely about sports.

I'd learned, by crunching all the data, that what worked on the internet was what I called SOFA: smart, original, funny, and authentic content. So long as we consistently delivered on those fronts, we would continue to grow the site.

By the end of that football season—Florida State beat Auburn to win the national title and end the SEC's seven straight years of title runs—I could reflect that 2013 had been the best year of my professional career. My national profile in media, to the extent that I had one at all, was the guy who ran OutKick and loved college football.

If I was considered to be controversial at all, and I really wasn't, it was probably because I ran a site that was willing to run stories like Manziel dancing with hot girls out at a college bar.

With OutKick, a Fox Sports contract, and a radio show, I was officially a major leaguer, not an all-star, probably, but an everyday player in the big leagues. I'd gotten my call up from Triple A, and I'd managed to hang around.

Politically, and I've said and written all this before, I'd been a moderately left-of-center guy. I believed in free speech and didn't care if anyone's feelings were ever hurt, but I was most assuredly a capitalist. In running a small business, I'd seen all the highs and lows that came with that challenge. But I'd continued to vote the way I had as a kid; I voted Democrat, for John Kerry in 2004, as a young lawyer, and for Barack Obama in 2008 and 2012.

I'd been working so hard at my jobs and with my young kids that I hadn't really spent that much time worried about larger issues in politics. After all, I did sports. What did I care who you voted for or what your politics were?

The next year, I hosted a Friday night show for Fox Sports on FS1, a preview for the weekend of upcoming college football games, live from the Fox Los Angeles studios.

At this point the first ten years of my career in sports media were, almost exclusively, about sports. Sure, we all argued, but the arguments were the kind of debates sports fans have been having since time immemorial: Who is the greatest of all time? Who is the most talented? Who is the best individual or team at a sport? In fact, here's an argument I think is true: Sports are the only thing people can argue about that makes everyone involved in the argument like everyone else *more*! I don't think that's true of any other argument about any other subject.

Sports were a unifier, and, in general, OutKick and all other sports media companies made people like sports more. For almost everyone, sports were a welcome escape from the real world, a place of refuge in times of conflict and struggle. Surely that would always be the case, right?

I thought so.

But starting in 2014, I was about to be proven incredibly wrong.

Because sports were about to become the vanguard of left-wing politics, and that would all begin, innocently enough, with a gay football player attempting to make it in the NFL.

CHAPTER 2

Identity Politics Takes Over Sports

I N 1976 BRUCE JENNER BECAME an American hero when he won the decathlon at the Summer Olympics in Montreal, setting an all-time record in the process, a record so profound that it would stand until 1991.

As he celebrated his Olympic gold medal, Jenner draped himself in an American flag, becoming one of the first athletes to make this a trend and captivating the nation in the process. He won the AP male athlete of the year award, appeared on the covers of *Sports Illustrated* and *GQ*, and even received his own Wheaties cereal-box cover.

Jenner would eventually marry three times, the final time to Kris Jenner, already the mother of Kim, Kourtney, and Khloe Kardashian, with whom he would have two daughters, Kylie and Kendall. Bruce experienced a new round of fame on the Kardashian reality show and by the mid-2010s, he was mostly known, if at all, as the loving father of the Kardashian reality show clan.

His sports background to a large extent was forgotten.

Until, that is, 2015, when Bruce announced he was transitioning to a woman and would henceforth be known as Caitlyn Jenner.

The announcement was a blockbuster, coming as it did on *20/20*, the ABC News program, in a sit-down interview with Diane Sawyer. The interview was a monster hit, producing 20.7 million viewers. What's more, I believe, still to this day, that the ABC interview also came with a promise from Disney, the parent company of ESPN, of a primetime ESPY award for bravery, which would come a month later on July 15, 2015. While Disney denies that they made this deal, Jenner's ESPY award for bravery became the first ever ESPY award to air on ABC and ESPN as a simulcast. Disney and ESPN rolled out the promotional red carpet for Jenner to a degree never seen or equaled before.

Now for those of you who don't know, the ESPY awards— Excellence in Sports Performance Yearly Awards is the official name—were founded in 1993 as a sports awards show for ESPN. It's their equivalent of the Oscars, the Grammys, or the Emmys. It was an excuse for ESPN to bring together its on-air talent and many top sports performers and throw a big party in July, typically on the one day a year when there are no MLB, NFL, NHL, or NBA games airing, during the Major League Baseball All-Star break.

Many awards are given, but the culmination of the night's cere- monies comes when the Arthur Ashe Courage Award is presented to a deserving recipient. According to ESPN, the Ashe award is for those recipients "possessing strength in the face of adversity, courage in the face of peril and the willingness to stand up for their beliefs no matter what the cost."

Ashe, a former tennis player who died of AIDS he contracted through blood transfusions, was first memorialized via the award in 1993, when Jim Valvano, the national championship—winning basketball coach of North Carolina State, took the stage to accept the award just two months before he would die of cancer. Valvano's memorable speech, which will bring tears to any sports fan's eyes to this day, encouraged everyone to never give up and promoted his V Foundation, which was founded to fund cancer research.

Subsequent honorees of the Ashe award have included the Flight 93 passengers, who helped bring down the fourth hijacked plane on 9/11, former Arizona Cardinals safety Pat Tillman, who left the NFL to serve his country and died in combat, former MLB player Steve Palermo, who became paralyzed fighting back against a mugger, Nelson Mandela, Muhammad Ali, and Pat Summitt, legends of the sports and political world, by and large, whose heroism is without question.

I don't recall any of these choices being particularly controversial at all.

But the year before they awarded Caitlin Jenner the ESPY, ESPN stepped right into the culture wars, awarding Michael Sam, the first openly gay NFL player, the Arthur Ashe Courage Award in the summer of 2014. Over a decade later, with the clarity of hindsight, the lionizing of Sam may well have been the first sign of sports going woke. In particular, there was a controversy surrounding Sam's drafting in the spring of 2014, when ESPN kept a camera on him and then showed Sam kissing his boyfriend in the immediate aftermath of his late-round selection.

At the time, I felt the coverage was gratuitous and excessive, not because Sam was gay but because Sam wasn't a particularly high draft pick. He went 249th overall in the seventh round, one of the final picks overall that year—and most of the time noncelebrity college players who aren't high draft picks are mostly ignored by the media and fans. In fact, Sam's performance at the NFL combine had raised many questions. He was seen as too slow to play linebacker and not big enough to play defensive end, a classic tweener, someone who may succeed in college but doesn't have an ideal home in the NFL.

NFL scouts turned out to be correct.

Sam never played in a regular season NFL game. Cut by the St. Louis Rams, he eventually played in the Canadian Football League before retiring from the sport. His brief fame was entirely connected to his sexuality, having virtually nothing to do with his football talents. And this was, I believe, the first true instance of identity politics capturing sports in the social media age. Sam's athletic talents had virtually nothing to do with the attention he received. He was the first athlete I can recall dominating sports coverage without ever dominating sports at all.

Since this time there have been other football players announce they were gay—some of whom have played in regular season NFL games—but the general reaction from football fans has been mostly indifference. For better or worse, despite ESPN's infatuation with identity politics and sports, most fans don't care at all about a player's sexuality. All they care about is performance on the field.

So Sam's ESPY for bravery and the excessive coverage of his on-field NFL preseason performance based on his sexuality was a tipping point. But at least Sam's connection to the sport was real: He was gay and a current NFL player.

It was, however, an important test case, the first time a player was covered by sports media based on his identity, not his actual sports talent.

Significantly, it's impossible to ignore that the pivot to identity politics in 2014 occurred as Twitter took over the national discourse in sports. To me the collapse of sports as a unifying source across race, sex preference, gender, and political divides is inextricably intertwined with the rise of social media. It wasn't just, as we have certainly discovered, that most members of the sports media were on the far left and having social media accounts emboldened them to be even more so. It was that traditional boundaries vanished overnight. Where once, for better or worse, sports debates had entirely focused on a player's on-field or on-court performance, social media expanded the arena to encompass a player's identity and their politics, two things that had nothing to do with success or failure in athletics.

Identity politics had made a run at sports before in the twenty-first century: Notably in the Duke Lacrosse case of 2006, when mostly white male lacrosse players were falsely accused of raping black strippers. But that was in a pre–social media era. That story still, to a large degree, played out in the papers and on television. We hadn't yet reached social media mobs and the apex of cancel culture. But I would argue the Duke Lacrosse case was the first time the massive political divide between the average sports media member, who was far left wing, and the average sports fan, who tended to be apolitical and probably a bit right of center, truly was exposed.

Of course, the Duke Lacrosse case wasn't the first sports story to collide with race, politics, and socioeconomics either. The entire O. J. Simpson case in the 1990s—black man kills white woman and white man and gets away with it in the aftermath of the Rodney King beating case—was also an example of identity politics intersecting with sports. But both of those were criminal cases colliding with sports. And, again, they both predated the social media era and weren't directly connected to the on-field experience itself.

Plus, whatever you thought of these criminal cases, the media, typically through television, radio, and print, drove all the coverage. Very often in social media, it was television, radio, and print chasing the online mobs.

The best historic analogy for what we were entering in 2014 was an echo of the late 1960s, when sports had become political during the civil rights era and the Vietnam War, which is why Jenner's lionization in the 1976 Olympics served as a patriotic response to the black power fists raised in the air at the 1968 Olympics on the medal stand by Tommie Smith and John Carlos. Interestingly, in this take on the historical record, Jenner was both the end of and the return to the era of identity politics in sports.

But whatever you think of Sam's sexuality, he was, at least, a player on the field.

By 2015 Bruce Jenner, newly named Caitlyn Jenner, was mostly famous because of reality television, not sports.

And ESPN's decision to follow Michael Sam's Arthur Ashe award with an award for Caitlyn Jenner abandoned all pretenses. They fully embraced identity politics by awarding Jenner the bravery award in a primetime presentation that just so happened to be the very first ESPY awards to ever air on ABC, just a few weeks after ABC had broken the news of Jenner's transition to being a woman on ABC News's *20/20* program.

The award landed like a bombshell in the world of sports.

And, I firmly believe, it officially marked the launch of woke sports and the end of ESPN's huge popularity among sports fans.

A moment of definition here. What is woke sports, some of you may be asking?

To me the answer is pretty simple. Woke sports is any coverage of sports-related issues through the prism of identity politics. Prior to woke sports, most sports coverage focused on the best, most talented male and female athletes. That's not to suggest that an athlete might not be controversial in many respects and make news as a result— Dennis Rodman certainly was controversial for his entire Chicago Bulls career, but Rodman was also a phenomenal basketball player. Rodman's basketball talents made him newsworthy, and his outlandish public persona was directly connected to his basketball talents.

Michael Sam, a late-round NFL pick who never even played in a regular season game, was famous only because he was gay.

If he hadn't been gay, ESPN wouldn't have covered him at all. He wouldn't have been a story. The woke sports era is primarily defined by media coverage not based primarily on athletic talent but on identity instead.

Michael Sam was the beginning of woke sports. But Caitlyn Jenner, a retired athlete with no connection to modern-day sports at all, being given the top award on a sports telecast was the official launch point for the wedding of identity politics and sports. Suddenly your race, your sexuality, and your politics mattered more than your talent on the field or court.

(I wrote a great deal about the collapse of ESPN due to the network's embrace of identity politics in a prior book of mine, *Republicans Buy Sneakers Too*, which is a famous quote from Michael Jordan about why he didn't get involved in politics. Jordan didn't want to alienate anyone by focusing on his politics. It was the correct, and smart, decision since many Republicans, as you'll see in a bit, love, for instance, basketball and Donald Trump. But from this point forward, ESPN completely and totally lost its mind and allowed far left-wingers in the network to dictate all decisions. They rejected the Jordan rules and began to lead their sports coverage with left-wing politics.)

In picking Jenner as their new hero, ESPN served as a convenient idol from the world of sports for the trans community. Because by the time Bruce became Caitlyn, he'd been removed from athletic competition for nearly forty years. Seven years later, when William became Lia, he did so in the middle of his athletic career, literally switching from the men's to women's swim team at the University of Pennsylvania. By transitioning forty years after Jenner's athletic career ended, all of these difficult questions were avoided for ESPN back in 2015. But it is worth asking even today: What if Bruce had become Caitlin a year after he had won the gold medal for men in 1976 and attempted to return as a woman's decathlete in the 1980 Olympics?

Virtually no sports fans would have accepted this.

Heck, Caitlyn is a Republican and a huge supporter of Donald Trump. Indeed, Caitlyn is a zealous advocate against men being allowed to compete in women's sports, even speaking out against the idea of Lia Thomas being able to swim against women.

Yet by the summer of 2015, Caitlyn Jenner was a hero, celebrated on the stage at ESPN, the bravest of the brave, the equivalent of Pat Tillman or the Flight 93 passengers. People who had given their lives to fight terror were the same as a man who had decided to become a woman forty years after his athletic career ended.

Yet as Caitlyn Jenner stepped on the ESPY's stage, criticism from sports media was virtually nonexistent.

Because it wasn't just identity politics on the ascent. It was cancel culture on social media too. Everyone had begun to fear what might happen if the wrong thing was said. (In 2012, ESPN fired an editor for using the headline "Chink in the Armor" in a story about New York Knicks point guard Jeremy Lin. A sports anchor at ESPN who used the same phrase had also been suspended.) And, look, I get why so many in sports media, even people who weren't crazy left-wing loons, stayed silent as the woke sports era began to take over. If you were a middle-aged white guy who made a decent living writing about sports, did you really want to get fired for speaking out against the insanity? (The radio voice of the Sacramento Kings, Grant Napear, was fired in 2020 for simply tweeting "all lives matter" during the Black Lives Matter era. ESPN fired a white guy who called tennis matches, Doug Adler, for using the phrase "guerrilla effect" to describe Venus Williams charging the net in a match. The network thought it sounded too much like he was calling Venus a gorilla. Really.) If you had a mortgage to pay and kids to put through college, could you really afford to lose your job standing up to left-wing sports insanity? Most couldn't. So the left-wing tide of insanity only grew.

But something else interesting had happened just one month before Caitlyn Jenner's acceptance of the ESPY award for courage. Donald J. Trump came down the escalator at Trump Tower and announced his candidacy for president on June 15, 2015. The Trump era, and the woke sports era, it turned out, had almost identical birthdays. And while Trump's win in 2016 would accelerate the battle in sports, I'll argue in this book that his 2024 win effectively ended the Jenner-Sam-Kaepernick woke sports era.

But for me, and for OutKick, the sports world fundamentally changed in the fall of 2015, when protests came to the University of Missouri and directly impacted the college football season. From that point forward, identity politics and sports were inextricable. And, not for the first time, I just couldn't keep my mouth shut any longer.

CHAPTER 3

Woke Sports Rises

I N THE FALL OF 2015, protests on the University of Missouri's Columbia campus began. The protesters alleged racism had taken over Missouri's flagship university. The story exploded in sports media when the Missouri football team threatened in November of 2015 not to take the field amid a hunger strike and the campus quad was taken over by protesters.

Immediately upon the players announcing they would not play, what felt like every college football writer in America praised the Missouri football team for their bravery in standing up against racism. But I had a different reaction. Far from being racist, the University of Missouri felt like an incredibly welcoming place for everyone, regardless of race or sexuality, when I'd visited and covered the athletic programs. What evidence was there for the university being steeped in racism and homophobia? After all, Missouri had warmly embraced Michael Sam just one year before when he'd announced he was gay.

Put simply, having been to the campus and experienced the culture of the school, I just didn't believe that Missouri was a hotbed of racism and homophobic oppression. In fact, it felt like the exact opposite to me. So I did something pretty crazy for a sports website; I actually investigated and wrote about the racism protests and their allegations.

And it turned out to be almost completely made up and exaggerated.

The Missouri protests of the fall of 2015 were based on three alleged incidents of racial oppression:

1. The president of the student body, a gay black man, claimed someone had yelled a slur at him off campus from the bed of a pickup truck.
2. A drunk student allegedly used a racial slur while walking through a campus rally.
3. Someone, we never found out who, drew a poop swastika on a bathroom dorm wall.

That was the entirety of the racism and oppression alleged to have occurred on Missouri's campus. This was what demanded the football team refuse to play. This was what led to the campus quad being overtaken by student protesters.

Now, look, I wish nothing bad ever happened to any college student of any race on any campus. But I'm also a realist, so I know this goal is impossible. But I thought it was crazy that the entire University of Missouri campus was nearly shut down—and the football team nearly refused to play a game!—all because of three relatively innocuous and insignificant events, none of which are documented to have even 100 percent occurred.

I went to college in Washington, DC. I can't even imagine thinking back then that I should notify the campus police if someone said something mean to me on campus, much less if someone said something mean to me *off campus*. Yet that was what started this entire charade of absurdity.

And what scared me was how quickly the sports media covering college football all lined up to label these protesting students as heroes and the entire University of Missouri as racist. No one bothered to investigate the allegations; no one asked any questions. In fact OutKick was on a virtual island on this story by even examining any of these allegations and writing about them. Before it was all complete, the president and the chancellor in charge of the university would be forced to step down.

Based on nothing!

Eventually the protest collapsed, and now the entire incident is a distant memory for many, but the impact was very real in Missouri. Freshmen enrollment at the University of Missouri declined by 25 percent in the fall of 2016 in the wake of the campus protests. It was an early, prescient indication of the toll woke politics could extract on a university campus, yet mostly it was ignored by the legacy media.

Looking back now, Michael Sam and Caitlyn Jenner winning ESPYs and the Missouri hoax racial protests can seem insignificant, but I believe they were actually incredibly consequential because they all established an important benchmark. Only one form of coverage was allowed when gay-, trans-, or race-related issues intersected with sports: The gay, trans, and minority person was the courageous hero, and anyone who disputed this narrative in any way was a bigot.

Worse than that, not only were you a bigot but you deserved to be canceled. If you were a sports media member in 2014 or 2015, you were on notice: Applaud gay, trans, and black heroes, or your job was in jeopardy. (This was particularly pernicious because the direct statement here—it wasn't even implied, it was directly stated as the woke sports era grew—was that if you questioned any instance of racism, sexism, or didn't believe a gay, trans, female, or minority accuser, that meant you were racist, sexist, and transphobic yourself. That is, your identity served as clear and convincing evidence in the mind of the left and in the woke sports era that your story was correct, and anyone who doubted you needed to be canceled. The woke sports era used the history of racism and sexism in the past—which, make no mistake, definitely existed—as prima facie evidence that any accusation in the modern day was true.)

For better or worse, I've never been able to bite my tongue when it comes to saying what I really think. Sometimes that works out great—it's made OutKick and my radio shows tremendous media success stories—but sometimes that doesn't work out so great. I've been kicked out of my son's Little League game for disputing a call from the stands. (In my defense, it was *crazy* to call batter interference on a 2–0 catcher throw to third that had no impact on the game to end the inning with two runners on base in a one-run game.) In fact, the very first time I met my father-in-law, I was kicked out of a coed law school flag football game—my future wife was on my team— for calling another player a pussy because he objected to how aggressively a girl had grabbed his flag. I had to watch the rest of the game from my car after an intramural referee escorted me off the field. At my ten-year-old's flag football game this spring, an official missed two calls so egregiously—I legit think this ref might be blind—that I told him he needed to retire. (Seriously, you're getting paid. You can't be that bad at your job. I don't care how old the players are.)

Anyway, my point is I have no filter, and I'm unable to keep my mouth shut when I see something I think is wrong. That has positives and negatives. The positive is that I say what most people think but don't say. The negative? There's a reason most people don't say exactly what they think. Because speaking out can have significant consequences.

And make no mistake, I have suffered real consequences as I'll discuss shortly. Because when you speak out against the online herd, they do their best to silence you because your very existence is a threat to their homogeneity and their power.

The parameters of acceptable sports reporting had been established with Michael Sam and Caitlyn Jenner: Oppose woke sports, and you will find yourself unemployed. Which is why the table had been perfectly set for the ultimate woke sports hero when Colin Kaepernick's protest in the summer of 2016 came and blew up all of sports to a degree not seen since the 1960s.

This is truly incredible because by and large Colin Kaepernick is a moron who has said virtually nothing of any substance or intelligence in the over eight years since his protest began.

On August 16, 2016, before the San Francisco 49ers played the Green Bay Packers in an otherwise meaningless preseason football game, Colin Kaepernick refused to stand for the national anthem. After the game Kaepernick said he refused to stand for the anthem because, "I am not going to stand up to show pride in a flag for a country that oppresses black people and people of color. To me, this is bigger than football, and it would be selfish on my part to look the other way. There are bodies in the street and people getting paid leave and getting away with murder."

This was the totality of Kaepernick's comments on his decision, which he made, crazily, in the postgame press conference while wearing a Fidel Castro shirt.

To his credit Armando Salguero, then a writer at the *Miami Herald* and now a writer at OutKick, asked Kaepernick before a game later that season against the Miami Dolphins how he could claim to be advocating for minority rights while wearing a Fidel Castro shirt. It didn't go well for Kaepernick when he said Castro was one of his heroes. Asked why he supported Castro, Kaepernick responded, "One thing Fidel Castro did do is they have the highest literacy rate [not true] because they invest more in their education system than they do in their prison system [not true], which we do not do here even though we're fully capable of doing that. . . . We do break up families here. That's what mass incarceration is. That was the foundation of slavery, so our country has been based on that as well as the genocide of Native Americans."

After this mangled answer, Kaepernick refused to answer any more questions from the media, a stance he has mostly remained committed to over the past eight years. That was probably a wise decision since Kaepernick was also asked soon after his protest whether he was concerned that his protest might be seen as a "blanket indictment" of police.

Leading to this incredible exchange.

Question: Are you concerned that this is seen as a blanket indictment of law enforcement?

Kaepernick: What's that?

Question: It can be seen as a blanket indictment of law enforcement.

Kaepernick: As far as what? I don't really understand what you're trying to get at.

Questioner: You say people are getting murdered by police. You seem to indict all of police.

Legit, Kaepernick is a moron. He didn't even know what the phrase "blanket indictment" meant.

But the left-wing sports media covered him as a hero.

Even though, to this day, there is literally not one single exchange where Kaepernick comes off as intelligent or thoughtful. Yet the media narrative was set. It had been embedded a year earlier with the rise of identity politics. Any criticism of Kaepernick was racist. He was a hero; argue otherwise and you were in danger of losing your job.

I wrote about the fallacies of the Kaepernick protest in *Republicans Buy Sneakers Too*. But that book was written in 2017 and released in 2018 before Kaepernick made tens of millions of dollars on his protest, sued the NFL because no one would hire him, and released multiple documentaries about how racist the NFL was.

Most memorably, in a 2021 Netflix documentary, Kaepernick compares the NFL draft to a slave auction. As Kaepernick narrates, a slave auction from the 1800s morphs into a modern-day NFL draft, with slaves turned into football players on the screen as they walk across a stage. Kaepernick makes the analogy direct and explicit, stating, "What they don't want you to understand is what's being established is a power dynamic. Before they put you on the field, teams poke, prod, and examine you, searching for any defect that might affect your performance. No boundary respected. No dignity left intact."

"Look at this here! Come on! Who wants this?" shouted a white auctioneer in the Kaepernick documentary as he sold a slave/football player.

For those of you who are not aware, the NFL draft is a high-stakes job interview where players all over the country of all races compete to become multimillionaires. The top draft pick in the 2025 draft, Cam Ward, a black man, received a guaranteed contract of $48.7 million, of which $32.1 million was immediately payable as a signing bonus the moment he signed the contract.

To the best of my historic knowledge, slaves were not given multimillion-dollar signing bonuses to work in the plantation fields. If they had been, slavery probably would have been a far more fulfilling existence and, you know, not actual slavery.

The ultimate irony, of course, is that Kaepernick begged for years to be allowed to play football in the NFL again. Meaning, by his own logic, he sought to return to being a slave.

Plainly, Kaepernick is a moron without any true logic supporting his protests. But in 2016 his protest galvanized the woke sports universe. Other players followed his lead, kneeling during anthems too, creating a conflict between President Donald Trump, who had demanded that players stand for the anthem, and the players themselves.

The story dominated the 2016 and 2017 NFL seasons, leading to collapsing ratings and ensuring politics became intertwined completely with sports. Indeed the 2017 season Super Bowl champion Philadelphia Eagles refused to visit the Trump White House, further inflaming racial tensions and creating more division in sports. What once had been a unifying escape from the serious things in life had now become yet another form of political separation.

After *Republicans Buy Sneakers Too* was published, the Kaepernick phenomenon continued to grow. In fact, in 2018 Nike made the unprecedented decision to re-sign Kaepernick as a spokesperson and plan a shoe and apparel deal built around him. This represented a drastic departure from Nike's historic focus: signing deals with the best athletes based on their athletic accomplishments.

Never before had Nike made the decision to reward a political activist with millions of dollars' worth of endorsement money. At the time I criticized the decision as a repudiation of the Michael Jordan era. Why sign an athlete who wasn't particularly successful on the field and antagonized a large percentage of the sporting public to be one of the faces of your brand? It just felt like bad business to me. Indeed, I even said going woke would be bad for Nike's overall business and called it the dumbest move in the brand's history.

The Kaepernick brand campaign's tagline, "Believe in something, even if means sacrificing everything," was nonsensical and dishonest since Kaepernick actually made more money by protesting the NFL than he would have if he'd never taken a knee in the first place. I even went so far as to say buying Nike stock would be a bad idea based on their signing of Kaepernick.

How did that prediction pan out?

On September 2, 2018, the day the Kaepernick deal went public, Nike stock traded at $80.30 a share. As I write this book in late June of 2025, the stock price is $62.80. So if you'd simply bought and held the stock from the time they announced a deal with Colin Kaepernick until now, nearly seven full years later, the stock is worth quite a bit less than it was then. But that's not all: Inflation—thanks Joe Biden!—crushed the overall value of a dollar in 2018 too. So not only would you have lost real money on the stock but you would have also lost massive buying power thanks to inflation.

But that's not even all of it. During these seven years, Nike stock has woefully underperformed the S&P 500. The S&P 500 was at 2,871 on that same September day in 2018. At the time of this writing, it was roughly 6,000. So the top five hundred stocks in America roughly doubled during this time frame.

Nike got woke, and the entire company's stock value collapsed, substantially underperforming the stock market as a whole.

And it wasn't just Nike. EA Sports, which makes the popular *Madden* video game, decided to get woke too. They insisted on including Colin Kaepernick in the *Madden 21* video game, a full four years after he had last taken a snap in the NFL. But that wasn't enough for the woke *Madden* morons. They gave him an overall player rating of 81, which was a better rating than actual NFL starting quarterbacks that year: Kyler Murray, Cam Newton, Baker Mayfield, and Ryan Tannehill.

At the time of *Madden*'s release that August of 2020, EA Sports stock was priced at $143.99. Almost five years later as I write this book, EA stock is at $148 a share. So EA's stock price has stayed nearly the same over the past five years at the same time the overall S&P 500 has gone from 3,400 to 6,000.

There's a lesson here, I think, which we will expound on in analyzing the NBA and Bud Light, two brands that lit themselves on fire by going woke. And that lesson is this: As soon as your company becomes obsessed with identity politics, your brand is in serious decline.

Go woke, go broke, indeed.

At least in the case of Nike and EA Sports, the more your sports company worked to promote Colin Kaepernick, the worse your stock performed. Being a victim paid really well for Colin Kaepernick, but it tanked everyone around him in the world of sports. Eventually Kaepernick's protest moved beyond arguing that police were racist and expanded to argue that, as you saw from the Netflix documentary, the NFL was racist too. Kaepernick divided all of us by arguing something that was fundamentally untrue: that the NFL was somehow racist against black people, quarterbacks in particular.

Sadly, this turned sports fans against each other by injecting identity politics into the NFL equation. The NFL, while far from flawless, is close to a perfect meritocracy. The best players make the most money regardless of their race, sexuality, or politics. All that matters, for better or worse, is your performance on the field. Indeed, I truly believe that the NFL is one of the least racist businesses to ever exist in world history.

The truth is this: There has never been any business that has created more black millionaires than the NFL—legit none in the history of the United States. Given the fact that black people represent around 70 percent of the NFL players, it was hard for even the woke Kaepernick zealots to argue that the NFL was racist. So they decided to drag us all back into the 1950s, 1960s, and 1970s and argue the NFL was racist against black quarterbacks.

Which was just flat-out untrue.

In fact, the NFL, by embracing sporting meritocracy, the idea that the best man wins no matter what, has actually been providing abundant opportunities to people of all races at all positions for a generation or more. I'm not arguing, by the way, that black quarterbacks were never discriminated against. But it happened before most of the people reading this book were ever sports fans. In fact, there have been a whopping twenty-nine black quarterbacks drafted in the first round since 1999, including the first three picks all the way back in 1999, twenty-six years from the present day, over a quarter century.

I thought about this when Jalen Hurts won the most recent Super Bowl and ESPN described the win as "black excellence." Was Tom

Brady winning seven Super Bowls "white excellence?" Of course not. It was just plain old excellence, the goal that all athletes regardless of race should aspire to achieve. Indeed, Hurts was the fourth black quarterback to win a Super Bowl and the third different black quarterback to win a Super Bowl in the past eleven years. (Russell Wilson and Patrick Mahomes, who has won three, were the other two recent winners; Doug Williams won back in 1988.)

Back in 1999 three black quarterbacks were drafted in the first eleven picks: Donovan McNabb was the second overall pick; Akili Smith was the third pick; and Daunte Culpepper was the eleventh pick. That year was very significant because in 1999, the same number of black quarterbacks went in the first round that year than had ever been drafted in the first round in the history of the NFL to that point. (Doug Williams was a first-round draft pick in 1978, Andre Ware in 1990, and Steve McNair in 1995.)

Twenty-six years before this writing, NFL teams decided to invest their most important draft capital—first-round picks and the commensurate money, fame, and attention that comes with that—on black quarterbacks. And do you know how it was treated then? As not a very big deal! Because sports fans aren't racist. We all believe that the best players should be paid the most money. That's the great thing about sports. The meritocracy works. But identity politics doesn't accept that argument. They have to make something other than on-field performance the point of discussion. They have to make sports about identity, not excellence.

But it wasn't just 1999 either. It was all the subsequent black quarterbacks taken since then.

Consider this list. In 2001, Michael Vick became the first black quarterback to be drafted number one overall. Since then, Vince Young was the first quarterback taken, third pick overall, in 2006.

Then JaMarcus Russell was the first pick in 2007. Cam Newton was the first pick in 2011. Jameis Winston was the first pick in 2015, and Kyler Murray was the first pick in 2019. Then in 2023, black quarterbacks went first, Bryce Young, second, CJ Stroud, and fourth, Anthony Richardson overall. The next year, 2024, Caleb Williams went first overall, and Jayden Daniels went second overall. The first quarterback to be drafted in 2025? Also black, Cam Ward. (The fact that Shedeur Sanders wasn't drafted until the fifth round turned into another racial quarterback drama, but most sports fans shouted it all down, pointing out the first quarterbacks drafted in 2023, 2024, and 2025 had all been black.)

It's not just that black quarterbacks have been highly drafted and highly paid. It's that it has become so commonplace that most sports fans don't even think about race when it comes to quarterbacks at all. All most sports fans care about is *WINNING*.

Which brings its own issues. You can get away with almost anything off the field if you're good enough at sports. But that's true of everyone in sports. So long as your talent exceeds your problems, you're always going to be employed in sports.

Lamar Jackson, Jalen Hurts, Deshaun Watson, Kyler Murray, and Patrick Mahomes are all making in the neighborhood of $50 million a year to play football. If that's slavery, as Colin Kaepernick alleged, sign me up!

Lamar Jackson in particular is an interesting test case because the woke race baiters in sports media have tried to make him their shining light for racism. How in the world is he a victim? He was a first-round pick at quarterback and now makes over $50 million a year.

So what's the alleged racism? Criticism against him during the NFL combine, namely one or two scouts suggesting he should play another position because they didn't think he was going to be a good quarterback.

Racism, the usual suspects, screamed.

Except, two white Heisman trophy–winning quarterbacks also had the same suggestion made about them. In fact, one of them, Nebraska quarterback Eric Crouch, was actually drafted as a wide receiver. Crouch wanted to play quarterback in the NFL but was seen as being too small and not having ideal arm strength. But he was so athletic that teams were willing to consider him at other positions. As a result, Crouch was taken 95th overall in the draft as a wide receiver. Crouch never played quarterback in the NFL and even switched positions from wide receiver to safety in an effort to make it in the NFL.

A Heisman Trophy–winning quarterback switched to defense to try to stay in the league!

And it wasn't just Crouch.

How about Heisman trophy–winning quarterback Tim Tebow?

Many scouts didn't believe in him as a quarterback and suggested he should play tight end instead. Was that racism too? After Tebow didn't make it as a quarterback, he even switched positions to tight end and attempted to prolong his career in the NFL that way.

Was the NFL racist against Crouch and Tebow? Of course not.

Yet eight years later, when Lamar Jackson was drafted in the first round in 2018 and entered the league with many doubting his quarterback abilities despite his Heisman trophy win, racism was the allegation. But Jackson was actually the third Heisman trophy–winning quarterback to be questioned in this manner, just like Crouch and just like Tebow.

But did anyone mention this at all?

Of course not.

All these racism allegations did was divide sports fans for no reason. So much so that it took nearly a decade for Kaepernick's racism narrative to be defeated and the "End Racism" slogan to be removed from the NFL end zones.

As for Kaepernick by 2025?

He's pretty much vanished from the national stage.

Not unlike a prior athlete who refused to stand for the anthem. Does anyone remember Chris Jackson, who changed his name to Mahmoud Abdul-Rauf? Most of you probably don't. As a college player at LSU, Jackson was an electric sharpshooter, one of the best college scorers I've ever seen. Playing alongside Shaquille O'Neal, Jackson and Shaq created one of the best inside outside combos in college hoops history.

Drafted in the first round as the third overall pick in 1990, Jackson refused to stand for the anthem in 1996 because he said the United States had a long history of oppression and tyranny, pretty much the exact same argument Kaepernick made in 2016, a generation later.

But NBA commissioner David Stern, unlike NFL commissioner Roger Goodell, took instant action against Abdul-Rauf, immediately suspending him because he recognized the immense destructive power a protest like this could have on the NBA. As a result, Abdul-Rauf agreed to a compromise, he would stand and gaze downward during the playing of the anthem.

Years later, almost no one remembers that Abdul-Rauf was the original Colin Kaepernick. He's completely vanished from pop culture and sports history.

The same, I believe, is happening with Kaepernick today.

When I published *Republicans Buy Sneakers Too*, there was a huge debate about what Kaepernick's legacy would be. Many argued with me when I said he would fade into oblivion, just like Abdul-Rauf. They tried to argue that Kaepernick would be considered a hero later in life. As we approach the ten-year anniversary of Kaepernick's initial protest, that's hard to see happening.

Kaepernick destroyed everything he touched, including his own career. The NFL, Nike, EA Sports, all of them are worse off than they would have been if they'd never engaged with Kaepernick at all.

So too, sadly, are many young victims of violent crime.

There are thousands of young men, mostly minorities, who have been killed, I believe, partly because left-wing athletes chose to demonize police officers. The massive increase in our national murder rate from 2016 through the Covid era is, unfortunately, directly connected to this misguided argument that police were responsible for the death of young black men. In 2019, 16,425 murders occurred. By 2021, at the height of the Black Lives Matter movement, 22,900 people were murdered in this country, a twenty-five-year high.

Young black men, sadly, are almost always killed by other young black men.

Indeed, police don't even shoot black men at disproportionate levels. Take a look at *The Washington Post*'s database on police shootings: It indicates that 75 percent of all people shot and killed by police over the past decade have been white, Asian, or Hispanic. Yes, it's true that black people represent around 13 percent of the American population, but they commit rates of violent crime, murder in particular, far in excess of other races. In fact, FBI stats show black people commit over half of all murders in this country, so when you analyze rates of police shootings as a percentage of violent crimes committed, black men are actually *less* likely to be shot than other races are.

And percentages don't tell the entire story either. For instance, men commit roughly 90 percent of all violent crime in this country. As a result, men are far more likely to be arrested than women. But does anyone accuse the police of sexism?

The truth of the matter is that it's the police of this country who overwhelmingly have worked to help keep people of all races alive. Unfortunately, Colin Kaepernick's protest spread far beyond the football field, and almost everything it touched got worse. Kaepernick's protest, which was a logical progression from the identity politics era begun with Michael Sam and Caitlyn Jenner, moved the woke sports era directly to the field of play.

The woke sports infestation continued to grow, and, unfortunately, speaking out against it had real consequences for me. All of the things I wrote in the paragraphs above I wrote on OutKick and said on radio and TV in those days too. Many people weren't happy with it. I was urged to speak out less aggressively, even offered a TV show if I would just give straight sports opinions.

But I refused.

And the consequences were real.

In the spring of 2017, I received a call from my agent. Fox Sports was ending my OutKick writing contract and my TV contract too. As a result, I would no longer be paid by or affiliated with Fox Sports.

Despite having entered into a new three-year contract with me in 2016, they'd determined that I'd violated my contract and told me they were canceling my deal. My outspoken opinions and my unwillingness to change what I was saying publicly had cost me a million dollars. They voided my contract overnight.

I was told my opinions reflected poorly on the company and were too controversial.

And just like that, OutKick was back to being an independent sports site, and I was back to selling ads all over again. Six years after I'd founded OutKick, I was back to square one. All because I couldn't keep my mouth shut.

That was very tough, but I'd run an independent site before. I felt like I could do it again. But things got tougher that fall when I went on CNN to defend everyone's right to free speech and said there were only two things I believed in: the First Amendment and boobs.

Most of you have probably seen that clip, but if you haven't, I encourage you to look it up now. If you do, you'll see a younger version of me, sitting down for a CNN interview with Brooke Baldwin.

OutKick was having a moment. We were starting to break big news stories as an independent site. I'd just been on Tucker Carlson's Fox News show a few weeks earlier to discuss my breaking news story about ESPN pulling an Asian man named Robert Lee off the broadcast of a University of Virginia football game because they were worried about the connection to the Charlottesville protests. (Seriously, ESPN had gone so woke that they were troubled by the idea viewers might conflate a white Confederate General who died in 1870 with a current Asian sports broadcaster of the same name). And CNN had invited me on to discuss a sports controversy: Should ESPN suspend broadcaster Jemele Hill for calling President Donald Trump a white supremacist?

I was defending Jemele Hill when I used a phrase I'd been using for several months. Instead of saying I was a First Amendment absolutist, which most people didn't understand, I'd been saying that I only believed in two things completely, the First Amendment and boobs. It generally got a laugh and cut through the noise.

Plus, people got it!

I was satirizing the woke culture and defending the First Amendment by saying something that was a bit risqué. So I said it on CNN, and the host Brooke Baldwin lost her mind, deciding to be offended by the phrase and demanding an apology. I knew the interview had gone off the rails, but I also knew there was no way I was going to apologize for what I'd said. That would defeat the entire purpose of my argument.

Plus, it was ridiculous. Men do, in fact, like boobs. Was it suddenly offensive to claim so? Was cleavage a new invention?

So I doubled, tripled, and quadrupled down.

The interview immediately went mega viral. It was everywhere. It's probably one of the most viral interview moments in CNN history. Even today it goes viral all over again every few months on social media sites as new generations discover the clip.

The moment I finished the interview, my wife texted me from downstairs. "Do I need to put the house on the market?" (Sidenote: I've discovered it's almost always bad news when your wife texts you from inside the house.)

When I went downstairs, she wasn't happy.

Before the interview, I'd told her I had only one more bit of work to do and then we could take the kids out for pizza. (We had three kids now, ages nine, six, and two.)

But now I knew that wouldn't be happening.

I was the number one trending topic in the entire United States. And left-wingers were coming after me in droves. They were all demanding that I be fired from my morning sports talk radio show. OutKick's advertisers were flooded with complaints.

The legacy media pounced and tried to cancel me.

They argued I was racist, I was sexist, I was a misogynist, and that there was no place at all for me in media.

My morning sports talk radio show, OutKick the Coverage, which was only one year old, teetered.

It was a Friday afternoon, and it was possible I'd have no radio show at all by the end of the day.

My phone was white hot, text messages poured in, and I was the number one story on Facebook, Twitter, and Instagram. My father-in-law, traveling in Europe, saw the story as lead news on CNN International.

I was everywhere.

If you've never been in the center of a media cancellation storm before, it's pretty all-encompassing. But I was calm and calculated. I knew my critics were out to end me, and I wasn't going to let them.

I like the fight too much.

But more than that, I knew I was right. The people trying to cancel me were actually proving my point for me. I'd gone on CNN to defend the right of people I disagreed with to keep their jobs, and now they were trying to take my job for what I'd said on the air.

Julie Talbott, my boss at iHeart, had my back. So did my bosses on Fox Sports Radio, Don Martin and Scott Shapiro. For that, I will be eternally grateful to all three of them. I kept firing away on social media, did an OutKick show discussing the controversy, and refused to apologize for anything.

By Monday morning, I was back on the air.

Many advertisers had bailed on me and OutKick. And trust me, I still know their names, and they will never be able to spend a dollar on any show I ever control for the rest of my life. In fact, their competitors can still get discounts. But I still had my show, which only continued to grow from that point forward.

And something incredibly important had happened: I'd survived cancellation. The people who hated me and what I was doing at OutKick had amassed all their artillery and fired every gun at me at once.

And I hadn't gone down.

I was still standing.

And I was mad as hell.

And I was ready to make my enemies pay even more than they had ever paid before.

Earlier I said that I'm a bit unique because I don't have a filter and that there are good and bad aspects to that. I say what lots of people think but are too afraid to say. That's why I have the audience I do.

Sometimes that means the masses are with me.

But I'm also willing to stand alone when I think everyone else is crazy. And that's rare too. Most people would rather be wrong in a crowd than right all by themselves.

Which brings me to a story to finish out this chapter. When my youngest son was five years old, in March of 2020, just before Covid would shut down the Little League sports season, I took him to his first Little League baseball practice. The coach that day brought the kids on the field for the first day of practice. He took them around the field instructing them—they were all four or five years old—on where the bases were and what the bases were called.

He took them to first base, then second base, then third base, home plate, and the pitcher's mound. Then he would say the location on the field, and all the kids would run to it. The kids were doing pretty well with the bases, but then he said, "Go to the pitcher's mound," and every kid ran straight to home plate, following the one or two kids who led the way.

Except my son.

Who went to the pitcher's mound and stood there all by himself.

I couldn't have been prouder of him.

Everyone else followed the leaders to the wrong place, but he was willing to risk being the only person to be correct by going to the pitcher's mound.

There he stood, a five-year-old in a ballcap, all by himself on the pitcher's mound.

Covid would hit a couple of weeks later, and he never got to play that season of Little League baseball, which was ridiculous and I think had a big impact on the 2024 election, which I will discuss later, but I like to think he gets that stubbornness from me.

And I hope he keeps it for the rest of his life.

I'm willing to be the only one who is right or the only one who is wrong.

Most people aren't. They'd rather follow the herd wherever it goes.

And that's made all the difference in my career.

That's probably also why OutKick continues to stand alone and why I saw the NBA's woke implosion coming before anyone else did.

It's also a great teaching point. Isn't it amazing how so many people on the left value diversity in everything but thought? They want an entire world where people look different but think the same. Meanwhile I just want a world where everyone can say exactly what they think and are willing to do so no matter what the consequences are.

We are not the same.

CHAPTER 4

The NBA Destroys Its Brand

I N THE SUMMER OF 1998, more people watched a basketball game in the United States than ever in the history of our country.

It was game six of the 1998 NBA Finals. Michael Jordan's Chicago Bulls were in search of their second three-peat, their sixth title in eight years. And Karl Malone and John Stockton's Utah Jazz stood in their way.

Late in that game, Michael Jordan stepped back, lightly pushing Bryon Russell of the Jazz in the process, and dropped a silky jumper through the net to give the Bulls the win. Jordan's right-handed postshot pose is forever embedded in sporting lore, a champion on his final shot as a member of the Bulls' dynasty.

Just shy of 36 million people watched that game, a record that the NBA has never come close to matching for the past twenty-six years.

In fact, never before and never since have more people watched a basketball game in America.

That game represented the absolute apex of the NBA in American culture. And it wasn't just that game either. The six-game NBA

Finals that year averaged 29 million viewers per game. If you were a sports fan alive in 1998, chances are you and your friends were watching these games.

I know I was, and I bet you were too.

What about now?

These are the average viewership totals for the past six NBA Finals series: 7.5 million, 9.9 million, 12.4 million, 11.6 million, 11.3 million, and the 2025 Thunder-Pacers NBA Finals, which had just 10.3 million viewers.

Holy crap.

The first and second games of the 2025 NBA Finals actually had the lowest viewership for a non-Covid game of any NBA Finals game since Larry Bird and Magic Johnson entered the league two generations ago.

That's truly awful, but here are two stats that make this data even worse: The United States population has increased by 64 million from 1998 to 2024, and Nielson now counts out-of-home viewing in its number, meaning modern-day viewership is probably inflated by about 20 percent compared to the late nineties. That means Jordan probably had 40 million or more watching him in 1998 compared to around 10 million watching LeBron today, which means the NBA has actually lost around 75 percent of its viewership at a time when the United States population has added 64 million to the overall population.

Wow.

How is this even possible? Where did the NBA's tens of millions of fans go? And why is this probably the first place you've ever read anything about the NBA losing its fan base?

Well, I'll tell you. Those fans didn't leave basketball.

In fact, men's and women's college basketball are setting ratings records. In the spring of 2024, 18.9 million viewers watched Caitlin

Clark's Iowa Hawkeyes team take on South Carolina's women's basketball team. That's the most watched women's basketball game in history. And it means way more people watched the top women's college basketball game in 2024 than watched any NBA Finals game. In fact, *six million more basketball fans watched women's college basketball than any NBA game in 2024.*

I put that all in italics because it truly blows my mind.

If you had told a Michael Jordan fan in 1998 that in twenty-seven years women's college basketball would be way more popular than the NBA Finals, he would have called you crazy. I know I would have.

Yet it just happened.

And it's not just the women's game.

The men's NCAA tournament posted record TV ratings for the opening two rounds in 2025 too, meaning more people are watching college men and women play basketball in the NCAA tournament than have ever watched in the history of both sports.

So it's not just that the NBA ratings have collapsed by 75 percent since the Jordan era; it's that the overall viewership of college basketball has *increased*.

It turns out that people still really like basketball. In fact, college basketball is setting all-time viewership records. So how is this not translating to the NBA? How is the NBA collapsing as record ratings pour in for college basketball?

It's left-wing politics. Going woke broke the NBA brand.

I'll get to that in a moment, but let's pause and consider the NBA compared to the NFL now too. I teed off on the NFL some over their moronic handling of the Colin Kaepernick protest in the last chapter. That response clearly impacted overall league interest and viewership for several years. If Roger Goodell had pulled a David Stern and simply suspended Colin Kaepernick, like he did with

Mahmoud Abdul-Rauf, the moment he started his protest, I think the story would have vanished almost immediately. Instead it lingered for multiple years, dragging the NFL's brand down with it.

The NFL Super Bowl data reflects that I'm correct on this analysis.

In 2015, the NFL set an all-time Super Bowl viewership record of 114.4 million. (Twenty ten was the first year that over 100 million people watched the Super Bowl.) But after hitting a record high of 114.4 million, the number stagnated a bit: 111.9 million in 2016 and then the number fell for five of the next six years, all the way to 95.2 million viewers in 2021. My thesis: The lingering impact of the Kaepernick protest and the NFL's embrace of BLM led to a clear decline in Super Bowl viewership.

But by 2023, a rebound began. The NFL nearly equaled their all-time Super Bowl viewership high of 114.4 million from 2015, posting 114.2 million viewers in 2023, followed by two new records: 120.2 million in 2024 and an all-time high of 127.7 million viewers for the Super Bowl in 2025. The latter coincided with an Eagles win that saw the stadium erupt in cheers for President Donald Trump, who became the first president to ever attend a Super Bowl. (We'll return to that game later in the book, but for now let's pause at this number, the NFL's record-high viewership set in 2025.)

The most watched football game in the history of the United States, Super Bowl 59, posted 127.7 million viewers, and it just happened in 2025. But the most watched basketball game in American history happened in 1998. So it's not just the NBA losing ground in basketball, it's also losing ground to the NFL too. How have the NFL and the NBA gone in such different viewership directions over the past quarter century?

That's especially the case when you consider that the 1999 Super Bowl, the game that aired just eight months after Jordan's record-setting game-six victory, had only 83.72 million viewers. At that point in time, the NBA and the NFL had never been closer in viewership. There was a gap of roughly only 48 million sports fans between the two leagues.

By 2025 the gap had grown to a staggering 116.4 million!

That is, 116.4 million more people were watching the NFL's biggest game than the NBA's biggest games by 2025.

We pointed out above that basketball hasn't gotten less popular, but football certainly has gotten more popular. So how did this happen? How did the two biggest sports leagues in America go in such diametrically opposite directions over the past quarter century?

By the way, even the National Hockey League, which isn't exactly playing the most popular sport in America, just posted the most watched non-Olympic hockey game in the history of the league in February of 2025, when 9.3 million people tuned in for a Thursday night broadcast of a game between the US and Canada.

And tens of millions more even tuned in for an exhibition boxing match between Jake Paul and Mike Tyson. The Kentucky Derby and the Indy 500 both recently set multidecade TV rating highs too, so even these sports are surging on TV. Clearly, most sports, even in a cord-cutting and streaming age, are thriving. So why isn't the NBA?

I think it's clearly woke sports. No league has been woker than the NBA. And no league has suffered more consequential fan collapse. And while it's tempting to attribute the NBA's collapse to the players—and they certainly aren't blameless here—I think we're missing an important aspect if we only focus on the players, namely, the leadership of the league.

During the Magic Johnson, Larry Bird, and Michael Jordan era of the NBA, as basketball surged from the NBA Finals not even being available live on television in the late 1970s to the most watched basketball game of all-time happening in 1998, all in the space of twenty years, the NBA was (mostly) led by David Stern, for my money the greatest league commissioner of all time.

Stern ran the NBA from 1984 to 2014, and his marketing genius, to a large extent, was to promote the relationship between the players and the fans. Do you remember the "NBA is FANtastic" tagline from the early 1990s? Stern ruled with an iron fist, but he was a benevolent dictator who made his players fabulously wealthy.

You'll recall that Stern brooked no attacks on the league. He immediately suspended Abdul-Rauf as soon as his anthem protest happened, and he insisted that the players conduct themselves like businessmen, even mandating dress codes for games. But Stern's leadership featured extraordinary growth, and he left the league in fabulous shape when he stepped down in 2014 and was replaced by Adam Silver, his deputy commissioner.

Whereas Stern's foremost partnerships came to be his relationships with Magic Johnson, Larry Bird, Michael Jordan, and later Kobe Bryant, Silver embraced the new face of the league after Kobe retired: LeBron James. And the LeBron and Silver relationship—aided, abetted, and encouraged by woke NBA coaches like Steve Kerr and Gregg Popovich—was an unmitigated disaster for the league. Both LeBron and Silver took over a league gifted to them in an incredible position and proceeded to destroy the goodwill built over generations in a few short years.

Immediately on entering the league, Silver undertook five super woke moves that infected the NBA with the cancer of identity politics: He banned the Los Angeles Clippers owner Donald Sterling for life for making inappropriate comments in his private life, a decision that forced the sale of the team and brought modern speech police codes to the league. He relocated the NBA's All-Star Game from Charlotte, North Carolina, over a transgender bathroom bill. He completely bent the knee to China during a free speech debate connected to Hong Kong democracy. He replaced the term "owner" with "governor" after some players and employees complained that the term "owner" was too evocative of slavery. And he also embraced and endorsed far left-wing politics, culminating in the disastrous decision to put Black Lives Matter on the court during the summer of 2020 "bubble" season inside Disney World's campus facilities.

Every time he was faced with a fork in the road, Silver took the left-wing route. In the process, he alienated a huge swath of his fan base, many of whom, it turned out, loved basketball and Donald Trump. Ultimately Michael Jordan was right: Republicans really did buy sneakers—and watch basketball—too.

In particular, Silver's decision to relocate the All-Star Game from Charlotte, North Carolina, over a transgender bathroom bill—the bill mandated that individuals use the bathroom on their birth certificates—was a radical and ultimately foolhardy wedding of basketball and politics. By making this choice, Silver made the untenable decision to align the basketball played in a location with the politics of that particular location too. This threw into question the NBA's ability to play in any foreign country, especially China, which had a horrible human rights record compared to America's. How could the NBA, many reasonable sports fans asked, play in Beijing, China, and not Charlotte, North Carolina?

Worse than Silver's own left-wing political decisions, LeBron, who had taken no political positions during the David Stern–era NBA, suddenly decided to embrace woke politics himself, campaigning for Hillary Clinton in Ohio in 2016. After Donald Trump's

2016 win, he even posed with a safety pin on the cover of *Sports Illustrated*, a supposed way to show solidarity with those suffering in the wake of Trump's victory.

My own take on why LeBron suddenly embraced politics in 2016 after over a decade of simply focusing on basketball? LeBron and his advisers realized he wasn't ever going to catch Michael Jordan and decided his new model was Muhammad Ali. It was a marketing strategy to keep him relevant after his career ended.

Others could argue that LeBron had experienced a political awakening and wasn't able to stay silent any longer. But whenever LeBron speaks on politics, that becomes impossible to argue, at least in my opinion. Witness LeBron James attacking then Houston Rockets general manager Daryl Morey for supporting democracy in Hong Kong.

In 2019 LeBron bent the knee to China, addressing American media and ripping Morey for supporting democracy around the world, including in China. "I don't want to get into a [verbal] feud with Daryl Morey, but I believe he wasn't educated on the situation at hand, and he spoke. And so many people could have been harmed not only financially, physically, emotionally, spiritually. So just be careful what we tweet and say and we do, even though, yes, we do have freedom of speech, but there can be a lot of negative that comes with that too."

Ah, yes, that awful, infernal American freedom of speech. There certainly are a lot of negatives that come with our First Amendment, particularly when it's being used to address Chinese dictatorships.

King James continued, "I believe he was either misinformed or not really educated on the situation, and if he was, then so be it," James said. "I have no idea, but that is just my belief. Because when you say things or do things, if you are doing it and you know the people that can be affected by it and the families and individuals and everyone that can be affected by it, sometimes things can be changed as well. And also social media is not always the proper way to go about things as well, but that's just my belief."

LeBron, famously, never attended college, going straight from high school to the NBA. Morey, on the other hand, attended Northwestern and later received an MBA from MIT. While college and graduate degrees aren't always the best measurements of intelligence, who do you guys think better understands geopolitics in China: the guy with an MBA from MIT or LeBron?

And whatever you think about democracy in Hong Kong, does LeBron's opinion read to you like an educated and enlightened perspective? Of course not. That's why I believe LeBron made the intentional choice to embrace woke politics, to make politics a part of his brand, to directly attack the Jordan Republicans-buy-sneakers-too ethos.

The result of the flare-up with China over free speech? China banned the NBA in the country for multiple years and pulled much of the NBA gear off its shelves. At the time of this writing, the league has still never played another game in China.

But it's coming.

Probably soon.

And in the meantime the NBA is playing in the Middle East, including in some countries where being gay can be punished with beheadings. Whatever your politics are, that seems a tiny bit worse than a North Carolina bathroom bill.

An intelligent and forward-thinking commissioner would have seen this untenable conflict coming and avoided it. But Silver is not an intelligent commissioner. So he steered directly into the hypocrisy. As for LeBron, I doubt he can even spell "hypocrisy."

As if being on the wrong side of the First Amendment and democracy weren't enough, LeBron also, in my opinion, manufactured a fake hate crime outside his Los Angeles mansion when he claimed someone scrawled a racial slur on the mansion's gate. Despite voluminous media coverage of the allegation, the Los Angeles police quietly closed their investigation of the incident after the alleged slur was painted over before they arrived, and they discovered the cameras directly outside the gate weren't working to catch the "culprits." That is, they closed the investigation because they found zero evidence any crime had occurred.

The decision by the NBA and LeBron—the NBA's own version of Jussie Smollett—to bend the knee to China all while ripping American institutions to shreds set the table for the event that would destroy the NBA's brand: the summer of 2020 bubble season at Disney World.

It's now been over five years since the sports world shut down because of Covid, but a small refresher: In March of 2020, every sports league shut down over Covid fears. I remember this sports era better than almost anyone because I was hosting a national sports talk show for Fox Sports Radio at the time. And, brother, let me tell you something. Imagine doing a sports talk radio show in March, April, May, and June of 2020 for three hours every day and not missing a day *when there were no sports being played at all.*

Something remarkable happened then, by the way. Our listenership skyrocketed, and that's one of the reasons I ended up taking over the biggest radio show in the nation with Buck Sexton in June of 2021. (Rush Limbaugh, the most talented radio personality of our lives, died in February of 2021, opening up his three-hour show window.)

The NBA, desperate to return to play but also terrified of its players catching Covid, decided to play in a "bubble" at Walt

Disney World in Florida. No players would be allowed to leave the campus setting, and they would be tested on a regular basis to ensure that Covid didn't spread. The players would leave their families and live in hotels, and no family members would be allowed to stay with them.

All of the games would be televised from Disney's mostly empty gyms.

As preparations for the league were underway in May of 2020, the George Floyd death went viral on video and Black Lives Matter protests took over the nation. Suddenly all of us who had been told by our health officials that we should socially distance and isolate from everyone were encouraged to break the lockdowns and march in solidarity across the nation to protest racist police and racial injustice.

The NBA could have seen itself as a huge, and much-needed, escape from the real world. That's certainly what most wanted to see from their sports leagues while they were still all locked down with Covid. But instead of providing a unifying respite from an incredibly divisive time, the NBA decided that its entire purpose was politics.

Players played games in the bubble with "Black Lives Matter" emblazoned on the court and replaced the names on the back of their jerseys with left-wing political slogans including: Black Lives Matter, Say Their Names, Respect Us, How Many More, I Can't Breathe, Enough, Say Her Name, Vote, Justice, I Am a Man, Liberation, and the somewhat puzzling Education Reform.

I still can't believe this all happened.

I watched these games—there were hardly any sports being played then—and I couldn't even figure out who many of the players were because they had political slogans on the backs of their jerseys instead of their actual names.

It was the manifestation of the woke virus taking over our country. Sports had fallen.

Virtually every player knelt for the national anthem in protest of the country, and the games themselves also featured obsessive commercials encouraging viewers to vote, clearly against Donald Trump.

This culminated when multiple teams refused to take the court for playoff games after Jacob Blake, a man with a checkered criminal past, who was armed with a knife and attempting to attack a black woman in Kenosha, Wisconsin, was shot by a white police officer responding to the black woman's police call to protect her from a man she thought would harm her.

Subsequent investigations confirmed the shooting was justified, and Blake would later plead guilty to two criminal counts, disorderly conduct and domestic abuse, receiving two years of probation.

But that would be in the future. Back in August of 2020, the NBA canceled playoff games because players refused to take the court after a black man tried to attack a black woman, who had called police to protect her.

Craziest of all, WNBA players, most of whom were black, actually took the court in handmade shirts praising Jacob Blake, and NFL quarterback Drew Brees even practiced in a helmet with Jacob Blake's name written on it.

The sports world had gone completely insane.

By the time the NBA players returned to the playoffs, the American sports fan had turned off the league. The 2020 NBA Finals averaged just 7.45 million viewers, the least watched on record. And that was even though LeBron James and the Lakers were in the Finals. Sports fans were done with LeBron.

In the space of just over a generation, the NBA Finals with Michael Jordan had gone from averaging just shy of 30 million viewers to averaging just 7.45 million for LeBron. LeBron had lost 75 percent of the audience of Michael Jordan!

But it gets even wilder. LeBron's actual NBA Finals posted a lower viewership than a documentary called *The Last Dance*, about Jordan's 1998 championship season. Let me repeat that; more people watched a documentary about Jordan's 1998 championship season than the actual 2020 NBA Finals.

There's more though. LeBron wasn't done trying to copy Michael Jordan. He also made his own version of *Space Jam*. LeBron's *Space Jam: A New Legacy* opened in 2021 to mostly disastrous reviews. The movie lost tens of millions of dollars, did a fraction of the inflation-adjusted revenue of Jordan's movie, and was almost immediately tossed on the scrap heap of movie disasters. Produced by LeBron's Spring Hill Company, the movie added to the production company's litany of failures, rolling up nearly 100 million in total losses since its founding in 2020, according to numbers reported by Bloomberg.

For good measure LeBron posted a picture of a heroic Cleveland-area police officer who saved a young black woman's life by shooting her armed attacker, also a black woman, with the tagline, "You're next," implying the officer was similar to those in Minneapolis, who had been convicted of killing George Floyd. When others told LeBron the police officer, who happened to be white, was a hero, "King" James deleted the post and never addressed it again.

LeBron, who initially copied everything Michael Jordan did, still had one indignity left. Many, myself included, believed the reason LeBron defended China so aggressively after Daryl Morey defended free speech, democracy, and basic human rights in China wasn't entirely just about basketball; LeBron wanted his new *Space Jam* movie to play in China and was afraid if he said anything bad about China, the censors would ban it. So he bent the knee to China and sold out American values.

The result?

China still didn't let his movie play in their country.

And the hits keep on coming. The 2024 NBA All-Star Game followed the 2023 All-Star Game to post the two least watched NBA All-Star Games on record. The 2023 NBA All-Star Game was played in Salt Lake City and only 4.59 million people watched, an all-time TV viewership low for the All-Star Game. But it gets worse. The last time the NBA All-Star Game was played in Salt Lake City was 1993, near the peak of the Jordan era. That year 22.91 million people watched. That means the NBA All-Star Game lost a staggering 80 percent of its audience from 1993 to 2023.

At this point, there is no debate. The NBA, uniquely among American sports, destroyed its brand with woke politics. Now, to be fair, there are other issues for the league: load management, too many three-pointers, a season that drags on too long, lack of team and player commitment, all of these things are factors too.

But ultimately it was woke politics that destroyed the league's ratings.

And the NBA's bubble season of 2020 represents the apex of the woke sports virus infecting pro sports. No other league has done more to destroy its brand, and no other league has paid a greater price for embracing left-wing politics.

Adam Silver and LeBron James have destroyed the brand Michael Jordan and David Stern left them.

The only way to fix things? Destroy the woke virus in the league. Something that, ironically, I think I've even convinced Adam Silver to do. Silver was asked about state bills having to do with transgender sports rights, in particular the state of Utah, where the 2023 All-Star Game was played.

Remember that the NBA relocated the 2017 All-Star Game from Charlotte over the transgender bathroom bill in North Carolina. Well, the state of Utah passed two transgender bills far more consequential than that North Carolina bathroom bill in the run-up to the 2023 All-Star Game. Utah passed a bill that requires all high school athletes to compete as the gender on their birth certificates—that is, no boy can identify as a girl and compete in Utah athletics as a girl—and a bill that denies gender-transition treatments to minors.

Given that the NBA pulled its All-Star Game out of Charlotte over a gender bathroom bill, wouldn't these two bills, which are far more consequential when it comes to transgender issues, including one that deals with sports directly, demand the same result?

Silver was asked about it and said this, "There was no discussion about moving the All-Star Game from Salt Lake City. I think by us coming to Utah and demonstrating what our values are in terms of diversity, respect, and inclusion, I think we can have the greatest impact."

It turns out Republicans watch basketball too.

But I bet you've never seen these numbers or this story anywhere before. Because most in the sports media don't want to acknowledge it. If they had, Bud Light, which I will write about in a few chapters, might have avoided the disaster that would ultimately befall them.

But it's not just the NBA that destroyed itself with woke sports; ESPN followed them over the woke waterfall too.

CHAPTER 5

ESPN Implodes

O N MARCH 18, 2022, ESPN broadcast the women's college basketball game between number one seed South Carolina—coached by left-wing superstar Dawn Staley, who believes men should be able to compete in women's basketball—and the sixteen seed Howard. During that game's halftime, ESPN returned to its studio host, Elle Duncan, as she stated that ESPN employees would be having a walkout at their studio campus in Connecticut to protest the so-called "Don't Say Gay" Florida state law signed by Governor Ron DeSantis.

I say "so-called" because the bill didn't actually ban the word "gay" at all. It just provided a commonsense educational perspective: There would be no teaching of gender- or sex-related issues to kindergarten, first-, second-, or third-grade Floridians in public schools. That's it! All the bill did was ensure that young kids were just taught education basics and not taught about things that were above their grade level, like sex and gender.

As the parent of three boys, and a current fourth grader, this isn't remotely controversial. In fact, public polling showed that huge majorities of parents agreed with it, including a majority of Democrat parents. Notwithstanding this fact, the Disney corporation decided to go to war with Florida over this issue, filing multiple lawsuits in 2022 that it would eventually withdraw by 2024.

But that would be in the future. On this particular day in March of 2022 in the middle of a women's basketball game, ESPN staged an on-air protest. Host Elle Duncan announced that the ESPN employees initially planned to celebrate women's basketball and the positive impact that so many in the LGBTQIA+ communities had received from women's basketball. "But," she said, "we understand the gravity of this legislation and also how it is affecting so many families across this country and because of that our allyship is going to take a front seat and with that we're going to pause in solidarity."

Hysterically to many, ESPN showed the arena shot—South Carolina led 44–4 at the half over Howard!—and the play-by-play announcer, Courtney Lyle, said, "Now normally at this time, we would take a look back at the first half, but there are things bigger than basketball that need to be addressed at this time. Our friends, our family, our coworkers, the players, and coaches in our community are hurting right now, and at three o'clock, about eight minutes ago, our LGBTQIA+ teammates at Disney asked for our solidarity and support, including our company's support, in opposition to the parental rights in education bill at the state of Florida and similar legislation across the United States."

The game analyst, Carolyn Peck, then followed, clearly reading off either notecards or a teleprompter: "And a threat to any human rights is a threat to all human rights, and at this time Courtney and I, we're going to take a pause from our broadcast to show our love and support for our friends, our families, and our colleagues."

At this point in the game, the second half begins, and the announcers are quiet for the next two minutes.

It was a remarkable moment. ESPN had truly gone fully woke.

If you had turned in for a basketball game on ESPN, as many likely had, instead you got a political lecture and a moment of silence to protest a Florida bill that the vast majority of Americans actually agreed with.

The date here is important too. It's one day after the Lia Thomas NCAA swimming title aired on ESPN. The high watermark of woke sports had officially arrived.

For seven years, ESPN had been building to this point. Since they awarded Caitlyn Jenner the ESPY in 2015, it was one stair-step of absurdity after another. And here, finally it had culminated in this: the wokest moment to ever air on ESPN. A game without announcers. An on-air protest over a state law that simply mandated young kids weren't to receive education on sex-related issues. Politics instead of sports.

On a sports network.

Imagine what normal sports fans thought. Those not immersed in left-wing woke insanity. People who just wanted to watch a basketball game. It's still stunning to me that sports reached this point, where men could become women's champions, where on-air protests of state laws that the vast majority of sports fans, and parents, approved of had become real.

How did this happen? How did a sports company so thoroughly lose its way? Well, I think I've laid it out. It was a seven-year process, a warning of what could happen if identity politics infected your company. A warning of what the woke mind virus was doing to our country.

The NBA had fallen, women's sports had fallen, and now the biggest sports network in the world had fallen too. Woke sports had infected everything.

OutKick was the last sports site standing. We were like my five-year-old on the pitcher's mound. Everyone else had given themselves over to the woke virus. A man had just won a women's swimming title, and ESPN had stopped covering sports to comment on politics. Everything I'd been fighting since the moment woke sports began around 2015 had culminated in this.

And while ESPN giving over its women's sports broadcast entirely to politics was shocking standing alone, the fact that this would occur in women's sports didn't stun me. Because women's sports have, on balance, been even more committed to left-wing political ideology than men's sports. Now, to be fair, women's sports are, in general, nowhere near as popular as men's sports. But the two most popular women's sports, basketball and soccer, have, at times, produced audiences that compete with or surpass popular men's sports, sometimes even when they compete head-to-head.

The two most watched women's sports teams of the twenty-first century, beyond a shadow of a doubt, were Caitlin Clark's Iowa Hawkeyes women's college basketball team and the US women's soccer team. No other women's teams come close to producing the audiences of each of these teams.

Confession: I didn't see the rise of Caitlin Clark coming. That's not because I didn't pay attention to women's college basketball—my dad was one of the biggest Pat Summitt fans on the planet, so we watched every major University of Tennessee women's basketball game for her entire coaching career. But I never would have believed that more people would watch the women's basketball title game between Iowa and South Carolina than the men's title game between Connecticut and Purdue in 2024. Or that millions more people would watch the women's college basketball title game than any NBA game in 2024. But it happened. And OutKick was there to cover the surge of attention for women's athletics by covering the pregame press conferences for both teams in the championship, South Carolina and Iowa.

One of our OutKick reporters, Dan Zaksheske, asked Dawn Staley if men who identify as women should be able to play women's basketball. Staley responded as follows: "I'm of the opinion of, if you're a woman, you should play. If you consider yourself a woman and you want to play sports or vice versa, you should be able to play. That's my opinion. You want me to go deeper?"

"Do you think transgender women should be able to participate in women's college basketball," Zaksheske responded.

"That's the question you want to ask. I'll give you that. Yes, yes. So now the barnstormer people are going to flood my timeline and be a distraction to me on one of the biggest days of our game, and I'm OK with that. I really am."

Later that day OutKick also asked Iowa coach Lisa Bluder her opinion on the same issue, and she declined to answer the question, saying she would answer it after the season. Well, South Carolina went on to win the game and the title, and OutKick followed up with Bluder and the fourteen other women's basketball coaches who made the Sweet 16 that season.

All fifteen coaches declined to comment when asked if they believed men who identified as women should be able to play women's basketball. I want you to think about that for a moment because that silence is extraordinary. The most successful women's basketball coaches in the country wouldn't even answer the question of whether they believed men should be able to play their sport. That's how woke women's basketball has become. Only Dawn Staley would even answer!

I disagree with Dawn Staley's answer, but at least she had the courage to answer the question, unlike the other top fifteen women's coaches in the country. Now Staley's answer is woke garbage because she knows men are bigger, stronger, and faster than women. In fact, Staley herself credits much of the success of her program to having her women's players compete against male players on campus. These aren't, mind you, the men's players who are good enough to play on the men's basketball team. These are just average intramural players. And the men smoke the women.

The first women's basketball coach to begin this trend was the legendary Pat Summitt, whose Lady Volunteers players regularly scrimmaged against male basketball players too. Often, the women struggle to even get the ball across half court and set up their offense. If a college male basketball player ever quit the men's team and began to play on the women's team, like Lia Thomas did in swimming, that male player would dominate women's basketball, almost certainly becoming the greatest "women's" basketball player of all time.

Yet it's become such left-wing orthodoxy to support this insanity—every Democrat senator opposed banning men from women's athletics, and only two congressional house members voted for the bill—that many are afraid of admitting what huge majorities of Americans believe, including actual women's basketball coaches!

Indeed, in January of 2025, *The New York Times* polled this issue, asking Democrats, Republicans, and Independents if they believed men who identify as women should be able to play women's athletics. The overwhelming majority said no, including 79 percent of all voters, 94 percent of Republicans, and a whopping 67 percent of all Democrats. So what's happened here? How have Democrats decided that supporting men in women's athletics, even though the vast majority of their own party opposes it, is a foundational tenet of modern-day leftist politics?

I'll tell you: It's the toxic cancer of identity politics taking over sports even though huge majorities of Americans disagree with it!

Far left-wing Democrats have taken over the party and bought in to the oppression Olympics, the idea that your identity matters more than the logic of your argument. So a trans person is going to rank higher in their party orthodoxy than the opinion of a white man, for instance, even if the white man's opinion is far more rooted in logic and facts. That doesn't matter.

We'll come back to this in a moment, but in the meantime, let's consider this under the prism of basic competitive fairness. Sports are divided by sex, age, size of schools, weight of competitors, you name it, all in the interest of basic competitive fairness. If women and men competed in unisex contests, then not only would women win no sporting contests but they wouldn't even make most teams.

Consider this for a moment: Every single Texas State boys' track champion in 2024 was faster than the women's Olympic champion. If you consider basic track-and-field records, a fourteen- or fifteen-year-old boy is faster than the women's Olympic records in the 100-, 200-, 400-, 800-, 1000-, and 1500-meter races. And it keeps going: They also beat the mile, the 5000 meters, the 400-meter hurdles, the high jump, the pole vault, the long jump, the triple jump, the shot put, the discus, the hammer throw, and the javelin. Again, fourteen- and fifteen-year-old male athletes, all still minors and all only recently having begun puberty, are better than the greatest women's athletes of all time in track and field.

As we noted earlier in the book, Bruce Jenner competing as a woman would have been fundamentally unfair. As Jenner has noted too.

That's not because the women aren't talented; it's just because biology is real. Caitlin Clark, as talented as she is in women's basketball, couldn't make any men's college team. And I don't believe she would be able to start on most boys' high school state champion teams. In fact, after I shared my opinion that a good high school state champion boys' team would smash the Las Vegas Aces, one of their players, Chelsea Gray, called me a "dumbass."

At the time the Aces were the defending WNBA champions. And WNBA players were agitating for higher salaries. So I issued a public challenge to Chelsea Gray and her WNBA champion teammates: I would pick a boys' high school state champion team and let them play head-to-head against the Aces. If the Aces won, I would give them $1 million of my own money. But if the boys won, I wouldn't even take their money, I'd give it to the boys as a reward for their victory.

We reached out to the WNBA and the Las Vegas Aces to seek comment on the offer.

Neither the team nor the league would comment. And they still wouldn't comment even after an online sports book offered to put up the $1 million entry fee for the Las Vegas Aces. So their team wouldn't even have to risk anything; they'd just get $1 million if they beat the high school boys. Even with no actual money at risk, they still wouldn't comment on my challenge.

But the $1 million challenge immediately went viral all over social media and the internet. On TikTok alone six million people watched my video making the challenge public, tens of millions more watched elsewhere. The interest was so intense that I even put more money on the table: I would put the game on pay-per-view and split the money with all the participants. I'm not kidding about this. I think this game would be the most watched women's basketball game of all time.

And the betting handle would be huge.

I'd make the boys forty-point favorites. And I still think they would cover that number.

I believe it would be a massacre and the women would struggle to score at all. But some feminists disagree. Good for them. Let's play the game. I truly believe it would be the most lucrative single basketball game ever played in world history.

But the boys would destroy the best women in the world.

What's my evidence? Well, all the track-and-field records I posted above. But also we have an interesting test case involving the best women's soccer players in the world: The US Women's World Cup team lost 5–2 to a Dallas under-fifteen boys' youth team. Let me repeat this; a boys' team made up of fifteen-year-olds—not the best fifteen-year-olds, by the way, just the best fifteen-year-olds in Dallas, Texas—easily defeated the best women's soccer team in the world. If a team of fifteen-year-olds from Dallas could do this to the US women's team, what could the best team of high school boys in the country have done? I think it would have been 20–0, or worse. The boys would have had to eventually stop playing hard to avoid pure destruction of the women.

The same thing would happen in every Olympic sport in the world.

If there weren't men's and women's Olympic events, there would be no female Olympians in any sport. The Olympics would just be played by men. And so would every sport in the world. Women's athletics wouldn't exist.

So when someone like Dawn Staley advocates for men being able to compete in women's basketball, what she's really advocating for is the erasure of women's athletes, period.

Now, I don't say this to demean women's athletes. I didn't put $1 million of my own money up because I'm in the habit of losing that amount of money on bets. I did it because the "girl power" era moved quickly from girls should be proud of being girls to being a girl is better than being a boy. Now we're supposed to argue that girls are just as good of athletes as boys.

This is manifestly untrue.

Look, sports are fun because we can all argue about which team is going to win. We can all bet on it now, and debating sports, generally speaking, is one of those things that makes everyone, deep down, like each other more than they did before. My radio show cohost, Buck Sexton, likes to say that I trust college football fans in all facets of life more than I do non–college football fans. He's completely correct in this, by the way. I do. Because I believe college football fans, and sports fans in general, speak a common language. And everyone in a sports argument is respected. We all argue about who is going to win the Super Bowl and then we go play the game, and at the end of the game, we all gather to talk about what we just saw.

Sports are, in many ways, our last bastion of shared humanity.

In fact, a scoreboard is one of the last relics of American life that everyone across the political spectrum trusts to accurately convey reality. Think about it. If the scoreboard is wrong, everyone notices and works to fix it immediately. If a three-pointer is ruled a two-pointer, they go back and look at the replay monitor to make sure the call is correct. We check to see if two feet are in bounds or not for an NFL touchdown catch. We all trust the scoreboard to be correct.

And that's the way it should be.

We need more things we can all trust. But don't argue with me that a man should be able to play women's athletics and win a title. Because as soon as you ask me to do that, you're requiring me to lie.

To me, requiring women's sports to be played only by women is a basic issue of competitive fairness, no different from age limits in Little League sports. As a father of three boys, I've coached Little League baseball, basketball, football, and soccer games at some point in each of my son's sporting careers. As a result, I know that age limits are zealously enforced. And woe unto you if it's determined that you are playing someone too old for the league.

Do you guys remember the name Danny Almonte? Almonte pitched for the Bronx Bombers Little League team in the 2001 Little League World Series. Almonte, whose fastball topped out at seventy-six miles per hour—even more imposing given that Little League mounds are much closer to the plate than big league mounds—threw a perfect game in one series game and struck out a staggering sixty-two of the seventy-two batters he faced. He gave up only three hits in three starts and allowed only one unearned run. As a result, Almonte and his team became celebrities.

There was just one big problem. An investigation discovered that Almonte wasn't twelve; he was actually fourteen years old. Action was swift. Every game was stripped from the record books. Almonte and his coach were suspended for life by Little League, and social opprobrium rained down on Almonte and the adults who had allowed him to compete.

I didn't hear a single sports fan argue that Almonte was trans-age. If he identified as twelve, why couldn't he play 12U baseball? Every single sports fan in America was united in opposition to the rules of competitive fairness being flouted.

Parents, coaches, and teams all agree that cheating and playing ineligible players based on age is such a concern now that many Little League tournaments require parents produce the actual birth certificates of the children in order to compete. I know this because a couple of years ago, my middle son competed in a Little League tournament in Cooperstown, New York. My wife gave me the official birth certificate, and on its return to me by our coach, I lost it almost immediately.

As dads have been doing for decades now.

Let me be clear here. I'm not opposed to girls playing in boys' sports if the girls are talented enough to play. One year, our ten-and-under baseball team had a girl on it, and she was the best player on the team. A fantastic pitcher. Good for her. When I played Little League baseball, there were a few girls in our league even back in the 1980s. Good for them. If a girl is talented enough to play on a boys' sports team, that's the sports meritocracy at work, but don't sell me the idea that because of girl power grown female athletes are the same talent level as men.

Because every sports fan knows it isn't true.

A few years ago, during the Covid insanity, Vanderbilt University's football team needed a kicker because several players were out for positive Covid tests. In what I still believe was a desperate stunt intended to help save a flailing coach's job, a women's soccer player named Sarah Fuller was called on to play in the football game. Fuller gave a halftime speech to the team that was trailing 21–0—really, that happened—and then came out for the opening kickoff of the second half. Her wobbly, short, bedraggled kick, which was legitimately the worst kickoff I've ever seen in a Southeastern Conference football game, was heralded as a momentous event for women's athletics, earning her—and I can't believe this is real either—SEC cospecial teams player of the week honors.

Vanderbilt went on to lose the game 41–0, the head coach was fired, and Fuller returned the next week to kick two extra points in a 42–17 loss that ended Vanderbilt's season at 0–9. Her jersey now hangs in the College Football Hall of Fame, and in 2021 Fuller participated in one of Joe Biden's inaugural events by introducing Kamala Harris.

The entire story was a ridiculous charade, but it was evidence of the continuing creep of the girl power and girlboss narrative, which many men, and increasing numbers of women too, find quite tiresome.

Perhaps nothing better epitomizes the tiresome wedding of girl power and sports than the trajectory of the US women's soccer team, which has gone from among the most beloved teams in America to one of the most polarizing during the Donald Trump era. For those of you not well-versed in the US women's soccer team, they burst onto the American sporting scene in 2015 by winning the women's World Cup title. American sports fans fell in love with Alex Morgan, Abby Wambach, Megan Rapinoe, Christen Press, and others. The US women's team beat Japan—I was in Vancouver watching the game with my family on our summer vacation—and over 20 million television viewers were captivated by the team's victory.

But then Trump was elected.

And many players, led by Megan Rapinoe, went intensely political. Rapinoe, in particular, began kneeling during the national anthem and denigrating Trump in her public commentary. In my opinion, kneeling during the national anthem while representing the United States in competition shouldn't be permitted. I'm all for free speech, but you don't have the right to be paid millions of dollars throughout your career to represent our country in international competition and not have the decency to stand for the anthem.

By 2019, this time with the women's World Cup games in France, the US women chose to disparage Trump and the United States on the global stage. Rapinoe referred to Trump as a "fucking joke." When the women won the World Cup for a second straight time, they refused an invitation to visit the White House to celebrate the achievement.

Rapinoe explained the decision not to visit the White House as follows: "Thanks but no thanks. I'm not going to the fucking White House." Later, she offered further explanation: "I wouldn't say that we're antiauthority, but when there's a person who is abusing their power or manipulating people, whether it's a teacher when I was younger or Donald Trump now, there's nothing that fires me up and grinds my gears more. I was just like: 'No. That's not happening.'"

As an aside, the US women's attack on the United States was particularly disappointing because the women of the United States, when it comes to sports, are uniquely privileged. In fact, you can nearly predict the winners of every women's World Cup soccer match by simply analyzing basic human rights in their home country. Women in democratic countries, mostly Western, with basic human rights are given opportunities that many women around the world aren't. The most uplifting possible message from star athletes from the United States is to point out that the reason they excel is because of American exceptionalism—that is, all women should have the same basic human rights, to pursue education and sporting excellence, as they do.

Instead, the US women's soccer team returned to America to file lawsuits demanding more pay. Women's soccer players make a fraction of men's soccer players around the world because the women's World Cup has a tiny fraction of the viewership compared to the men's. The United States, far from being worthy of ridicule, actually pays and supports women's athletics better than almost any country in the world.

Just imagine if that had been the message the US women had chosen to share. Instead, the US women got intensely political, culminating in the 2023 World Cup, where many American sports fans were actively rooting against our own soccer team. Indeed, when Megan Rapinoe, who had performed spectacularly in the 2019 World Cup, shanked a penalty kick, missing wide right, ironically, as the US women were upset by Sweden, many American sports fans exulted.

Trump immediately weighed in: "The 'shocking and totally unexpected' loss by the U.S. Women's Soccer Team to Sweden is fully emblematic of what is happening to our once great Nation under Crooked Joe Biden," Trump posted on Truth Social. "Many of our players were openly hostile to America—No other country behaved in such a manner, or even close. WOKE EQUALS FAILURE. Nice shot Megan, the USA is going to Hell!!! MAGA"

Not content with alienating tens of millions of American sports fans who would have otherwise supported her, Rapinoe responded to the end of her soccer career by endorsing the idea that men identifying as women should be able to compete in women's athletics. "Absolutely," she said when asked if men should be allowed to play on the US women's soccer team, even if that meant replacing current women. "You're taking a 'real woman's place,' that's the part of the argument that's still extremely transphobic. I see trans women as real women. What you're saying automatically in the argument—you're sort of telling on yourself already—is you don't believe these people are women. Therefore, they're taking the other spot. I don't feel that way." That's awfully convenient for Rapinoe. Just as her career ended, she endorsed the idea of men replacing women in women's soccer. While Caitlin Clark hasn't publicly made any comment on the issue yet, she did recently acknowledge her "white privilege," which feels like a step in the direction of woke progressivism.

Ultimately it feels to me like a man playing women's basketball or soccer, and dominating, may be necessary to end this issue once and for all. I base that on the impact that Lia Thomas had in swimming. Let's be honest. Swimming isn't the most popular sport, particularly at the college level. It was only Lia Thomas's decision to swim—and the resulting domination a male swimmer competing in women's sports produced—that created the societal backlash. (I credit my friends Riley Gaines and Paula Scanlan, as will be discussed later in more detail, with speaking out on this issue and refusing to allow it to fade.) But a man playing women's basketball or soccer would be impossible to ignore. As would his domination. (If a male player who started in soccer or basketball for a men's team announced he was a woman, that male player would immediately become the greatest "women's" soccer or basketball player of all time.)

When this eventually happens—it feels like a question of "when" far more than a question of "if"—the basic biological differences between men and women will become impossible to avoid. And the natural inclination of women to allow this competition to occur—remember that there are no Lia Thomas's in men's sports and there's no woman becoming a man even making men's sports teams, or certainly, being named the man of the year—means that ultimately every woman will need to make their voice heard on this issue.

But men, importantly, think men in women's sports is complete and total bullshit. And all of this woke insanity building up was creating a backlash. I could see it online in the comments to my $1 million challenge. Unlike Megan Rapinoe, young men and sports fans weren't willing to lie to further their political ideology.

Indeed, you could see this reality reveal itself in the late spring of 2025 when Simone Biles attacked Riley Gaines, seemingly endorsing men in women's sports, and then quickly backpedaled after she was deluged in ridicule. This is a real cultural battle for sanity that we have won in the world of sports.

So far this book has primarily focused on sports and the impact of the woke era on those sports. This is important because I believe the foundation of Trump's electoral victory came from men finally getting fed up with the absurdity that woke sports was demanding they embrace.

Sports act, I truly believe, as the gatekeeper of modern male culture because sports are uniquely important to men, both young and old. It's where young men for generations have gone to measure themselves on fields of play and admire, revere, and celebrate the best athletes.

If you grew up and are around my age, you probably had Bo Jackson and Michael Jordan posters hanging on your walls. I know I did.

I saw all of this craziness in sports, saw the audience growing for our OutKick site and shows, saw the enthusiasm for the Clay and Buck radio show, and felt the growing red tide of opposition forming against the idea that men could win women's sports titles.

And with all that in mind, I confidently predicted a red wave in the 2022 midterm elections.

And I was completely wrong.

Because it turned out that while I was correct that the high tide of woke sports had arrived in 2022, most people hadn't felt the wave yet. It would take the balls of Donald Trump to make it happen, to make the Lia Thomas story impossible to ignore.

So while I was frustrated the red wave didn't arrive in 2022, I still felt like it was coming. I had been so close to the story that I saw and felt the peak before others did. But I could see others would soon catch the red wave because it was happening in my own household.

CHAPTER 6

Girl Power

WHEN HE WAS NINE YEARS OLD, I took my middle son
to Target to shop for baseball and football cards.

It was during the Covid era, and my boys were obsessed with
baseball and football cards. Target had a small collection of rotating cards for sale, and one of my boys' favorite things to do was see
if any new cards had been put out at the store.

When we walked into the store, my middle son rolled his eyes
and said, "They'd never have those for us, Dad." I wasn't aware of
what he was talking about. "What do you mean?" I asked.

"Those," he said, pointing straight ahead at the display racks in
a suburban Target near our home.

An entire section of the front of the store was filled with "Girl
Power" T-shirts in all colors. "They would never have," he said,
"shirts that said 'Boy Power' on them."

He was right.

As the father of three boys, I'd never stopped to consider the
world they were being raised in—three boys coming of age in

the "girl power," "slay queen," "boss bitch," "you go girl" world. Young girls were constantly being taught they were special and possessed unique talents and gifts because of their gender. Young boys were, at best, ignored. At worst, they were blamed for everything that had ever gone wrong in the history of the world. Especially young white kids since white men, in the identity politics universe we now lived in, bear the foremost responsibility for every evil that has ever existed in the history of the world.

(Straight white men are the great Satan of identity politics; trans black men or women are probably its saviors. Everyone else is somewhere in between.)

Not long after this Girl Power shirt observation, another of my son's friends was at the house talking about the latest subject of woke instruction at their school. "I'm so tired," a preadolescent boy told me, "of hearing that boys ruin everything and we have all this power. My mom doesn't even let me pick what I want to eat for dinner, Mr. Clay," he said. "What power do I have?!"

Now these two stories are merely anecdotes. They aren't necessarily dispositive of larger societal trends. But as a dad of three boys, I think about the world they're being raised in all the time. Every child grapples with the transition from childhood to adulthood, but I do think twenty-first-century boys are under assault in a way that most haven't really considered.

I'm not an expert on kids, but I do think, in general, I understand what boys aspire to as they age into grown men. Every young boy wants to be bigger, stronger, and faster than he actually is. This is why young boys love superhero movies, why kids have athlete posters on their walls, and why athletic achievement matters so much to young men. Not all young boys, but most of them, at some point in time, have fantasized about becoming professional athletes.

And it doesn't change that much for grown men either.

Look at what grown men watch on television. It's generally sporting contests, stories about badass men (superheroes or action-movie heroes), or reality television featuring men engaging in extremely dangerous pursuits (driving on icy roads, fishing in dangerous waters, shark encounters). Men love Shark Week. The TV data is pretty clear: Most of what men watch on television, sports in particular, is aspirational in nature. Men watch men who are bigger, stronger, faster, and tougher than the average man doing things that are ballsier than what most men do.

Women, on the other hand, tend to watch shows featuring women who are crazier than they are. *The Real Housewives* franchise, for instance. Men, in general, aspire to be braver versions of themselves. Women aspire to be less crazy versions of themselves.

The deeper read here would be that men ultimately fear being pussies and women fear being crazy and that's also what attracts them to television, but that's probably too much Freud. My point is that most men want to be more masculine versions of themselves.

But what happens when masculinity itself comes under attack and what you aspire to become is seen, by much of society at least, as troubling? What happens when you tell men that they need to be a different kind of man than they aspire to be? Well, you create a generation of boys who are profoundly lost.

Which is exactly where men in modern society are today.

We've spent much of the past generation discussing how to ensure women have equal opportunities to men, so much so, in fact, that I think we've lost track of how to inspire boys. Consider this: Women earn roughly 60 percent of all college degrees now. For the past twenty years, most elite law and medical schools have enrolled more women than men, including my own law school, Vanderbilt University.

I remember going to campus interviews for jobs and seeing women were advantaged when it came to hiring practices because law firms had traditionally underhired women. But in my own class, the class of 2004, we had more women than men. If men were receiving 60 percent of all college degrees, it would be a national point of shame, a major discussion point for why women weren't achieving at a high level, a sign of our systemic misogyny.

But why does the failure of men to keep pace with women in college and graduate degrees receive almost no discussion at all?

In years past men were taught they should provide for their families, raise children, be the bread winner, be the foundational rock of the nuclear family. There's a reason employers, traditionally, have favored men with wives and children, because men are innately wired to take care of and provide for families. It's how basic biology works.

But what happens when suddenly masculinity itself becomes an insult? When toxic masculinity is discussed ad infinitum and the very concept of mentioning toxic femininity would be considered a hate crime? What happens when men are told that traditional gender roles are sexist anachronisms and that testosterone itself is a bad thing?

Combine all of this with a true dearth of men in households, nearly one in four children are now living with one parent at home, overwhelmingly the mother. That number includes, astoundingly, nearly 60 percent of black children.

Sixty percent!

Seventy percent of black children today are born to unmarried mothers. (That number is only 29 percent for white children).

And before Kamala Harris wants to argue that's because of systemic racism, these numbers have skyrocketed since the civil rights movement. That is, in the 1950s and 1960s, when racism was actually far more common, just 15 percent of black babies were born out of wedlock.

Add it all up, and young boys and young men today are profoundly lost. They're attacked as toxic by women and often left without father figures at home. Then add in the #metoo absurdities—suddenly young men had no idea what was and was not acceptable when it came to speaking with women—and the result is a profoundly alienated core of young men desperately seeking guidance.

And where would they find it? Particularly when so many of them were cooped up during Covid?

Online, often on YouTube and TikTok, located in the so-called manosphere of the internet. From Canadian philosopher Jordan Peterson—wear a suit, tuck in your shirt, embrace traditional notions of adulthood—to Andrew Tate—sleep with as many women as you can and get filthy rich in the process—men are desperately seeking role models.

But what they are learning from those male role models, far from being monolithic, is actually quite varied. Your son or grandson's role model online can be coming from a diverse panoply of online male influencers.

Before offering you a tour of this manosphere—that is, introduce you briefly to the individuals your sons or grandsons are often spending time with online—it's important to explain that this is not an exhaustive list. They may, for instance, watch quite a lot of sports. Most sports figures, however, are not really influential figures online, because their primary way of making a living occurs outside the internet universe, on fields of play and competition.

The individuals I'm talking about here have two important characteristics that unite them: They primarily exist on the internet, or at least founded their careers there, and they provide a worldview more expansive than what they do for a living.

Let me give you an example of four men who are incredibly influential for young men who aren't written about here as a part of the manosphere. Patrick Mahomes, Josh Allen, Lamar Jackson, and Joe Burrow are, in my always humble opinion, the four best NFL quarterbacks at the present day. All of them have tens of millions of online followers. But all four men make their living primarily playing football, not on the internet.

This isn't intended to discount their impact in the real world—all four men, I'm quite confident, voted for Donald Trump, by the way—it's just to point out that when people want to see these individuals, they turn on their television and watch sports. They don't pull out their phones and go to Instagram, TikTok, YouTube, or Twitter.

And none of these guys are doubling as life philosophers when they aren't throwing footballs. Athletes are influential, and athletes can be part of the manosphere, but no current athlete really is.

The groups that I'm breaking down here are uniquely online and have built their audiences through the internet. It's this group that Trump's team brilliantly targeted to move young male voters in their direction. But, and this is key, almost none of these individuals exist primarily in the political realm. In fact, it's their existence outside of the political realm that makes them so effective at communicating with younger voters.

And what all these groups have in common, at least in some respect, is they offer different models of masculinity, an attempt to answer the questions, What should a man aspire to achieve and how should he aspire to do it?

OK, with that background, I would argue there are six main groups of influencers in the manosphere, and they have a wide variety of life perspectives. But what they have in common is the belief that there's nothing wrong with being male. In other words, their uniting principle is it's OK to be a guy.

So let me break down all these groups for you.

The first group is what I would call the intellectual philosophers. This would be individuals like Jordan Peterson and Ben Shapiro. These men are fathers, highly educated, with elite intellects. I'll confess that I went to see Jordan Peterson speak at a private event in Texas, and his intellect, while stupendous, was often ponderous and complex, too ponderous and complex for most in the crowd to follow.

At the bar afterward, multiple people came up to me as we stood drinking beers. I remember one guy, a smart businessperson of considerable wealth and success, who said, "I think I agree with him on almost everything, but I had no idea what he was saying."

Peterson is, for many, an ambitious undertaking, the kind of person that saying you're a fan of brands you as being an intellectual yourself.

I purchased his best-selling book, *12 Rules for Life*, read the first few pages, and knew it wasn't for me. I'm motivated by story more than philosophy. Peterson is motivated by philosophy more than story.

What many men are seeking from Peterson is a purpose for their lives. In another era, one when religion offered many men their purpose, we had the Ten Commandments. They worked pretty well, generally speaking, if you could manage to follow their tenets. Here they are for all you infidels out there who have forgotten them:

1. Thou shall have no other gods before me.
2. Thou shalt not make unto thee any graven images.
3. Thou shalt not take the name of the Lord thy God in vain.
4. Remember the Sabbath day and keep it holy.
5. Honor your father and mother.
6. Thou shalt not murder.
7. Thou shalt not commit adultery.
8. Thou shalt not steal.
9. Thou shall not bear false witness against your neighbor.
10. Thou shall not covet your neighbor's wife.

As you can see, as a general rule, the Ten Commandments' first focus is on subservience to God and then the final six are directions on how to live your own life. As a rough life pathway, it would be humble yourself before authority and then manage your potential vices by abstaining from bad behavior.

But with religion collapsing in the country—although, interestingly, young men are now more religious than young women, and there appears to be a newfound religious awakening among young men in particular—Peterson's *12 Rules* now exist to fill the void for many. And those rules are almost exclusively focused on your own personal behavior.

Here are Peterson's *12 Rules*:

1. Stand up straight with your shoulders back.
2. Treat yourself like someone you are responsible for helping.
3. Make friends with people who want the best for you.

4. Compare yourself to who you were yesterday, not to who someone else is today.

5. Do not let your children do anything that makes you dislike them.

6. Set your house in perfect order before you criticize the world.

7. Pursue what is meaningful (not what is expedient).

8. Tell the truth—or, at least, don't lie.

9. Assume that the person you are listening to might know something you don't.

10. Be precise in your speech.

11. Do not bother children when they are skateboarding.

12. Pet a cat when you encounter one on the street.

By distilling a life philosophy into twelve rules, Peterson, a Canadian philosopher who had virtually no audience prior to 2010, now has 8.6 million subscribers on YouTube and 6 million Twitter followers. His best-selling book, *12 Rules for Life*, which has sold millions of copies, has a whopping 82,000 Amazon reviews.

Clearly, many people are seeking out the wisdom he provides, focused primarily on building a moral and philosophical guide to a better version of yourself.

I would put Ben Shapiro, who adds religious faith as his foundation, alongside Jordan Peterson on one side of the manosphere spectrum. Shapiro, a founder of the Daily Wire, is a deeply religious Orthodox Jew with a lacerating wit and a good sense of humor. Shapiro is also a powerful intellect, but unlike Peterson, who largely avoided religion as he became famous, religious faith and the morality embedded in Western civilization is Shapiro's calling card.

What I think people particularly love about Shapiro is he's smarter than most of his critics and offers a combative and pugnacious defense of conservative political principles without taking himself super seriously. (He released a rap song, for instance.) There are others you could put in this camp, but I think Peterson and Shapiro would reliably serve as the philosopher kings and intellectual heft of the manosphere.

The second group I would call the tech bros. Elon Musk would quite clearly be their avatar. Remember, this isn't really a spectrum of masculinity. In fact, it's often a Venn diagram of men connecting in some areas and disconnecting in others. And presidential voting itself isn't always a proxy for where these individuals fit in the manosphere either. Elon Musk voted for Hillary Clinton in 2016 and Joe Biden in 2020. He didn't endorse President Trump until the attempted assassination in Butler, Pennsylvania, on July 13, 2024.

Musk is, in many ways, a rational realist who views politics as a means to further his ultimate goal: making humans a multiplanetary species by setting up a colony on Mars. Musk himself wasn't even avowedly political for much of his time in public life. In fact, it was only a few years ago that Musk was considered a liberal icon because of his electric car inventions with Tesla. And that's part of what makes the manosphere so effective: The Ben Shapiros of the world are actually the exceptions. Most men who are popular on the internet aren't primarily popular for their political perspectives; they are primarily popular for something else first.

Musk's overarching goal, arguably, has nothing to do with politics. He's better at building spaceships than NASA, created a new way to propel vehicles without using gas, and only when both of these businesses, Space X and Tesla, were flourishing did he become concerned that the woke mind virus was a direct threat to humanity's ability to colonize Mars. That is, he bought Twitter/X primarily as a means to serve his ultimate goal: colonizing Mars.

Even his relationship with Trump, working to cut government expenses via DOGE, is primarily about allowing American
exceptionalism to win in the marketplace of ideas. Musk believes,
and I agree with him, that if the government embraces censorship, you are stifling human innovation, which ultimately detracts
from human accomplishment (i.e., sending humans to Mars).
There are many others in the tech-bro world, but Musk stands as
their avatar.

Musk overlaps to a certain extent with our third online bro group
in the manosphere: the online gamer and YouTuber. Chief among
them would be someone like Adin Ross, who gifted Trump a Tesla
Cybertruck during a Mar-a-Lago visit back in the summer. Ross
streams video games, and people watch him play in massive numbers. I don't particularly understand how this has become so popular, but gargantuan audiences of young men watch other young
men play video games, my own kids among them.

Some of these gamers and YouTube bros avoid politics like the
plague—MrBeast, the largest YouTube personality of them all, is a
great example of this. (I met MrBeast in a celebrity poker challenge
a few years ago, and my kids were more impressed by that than
anything I've done in my career. I'm not kidding. All three of my
kids have met President Trump. No offense to President Trump,
but all three of them would rather have met MrBeast.)

While streaming video games—clips of which are then made
and circulated online—these young men talk about things that
young men care about. That includes girls, sports, video game cheat
codes, and occasionally politics will intersect here. The YouTube/
gamer-pro power isn't that it's naked politics; it's that the politics
intersects, generally in an organic way, with the conversations
these guys engage in.

Far from making specific videos endorsing a candidate, their lifestyle overlaps with a candidate, and the candidate then visits in a hangout mode more than anything else. Trump, who spent much of his life hanging out in golf-club locker rooms before entering politics, is quite adept at bro culture. (You could argue a sports locker room is even the foundational location of bro culture in general. In fact, I would bet Trump has been having conversations like those in the manosphere today for most of his life.) As a result Trump and the advisers around him, often young men who live hyperonline lifestyles, was preconditioned to be able to understand this young male dynamic in a way Democrat politicians have not been able to. And even when Democrats do recognize their issue here, they misidentify the solution to their problems. This explains the entire dynamic with Minnesota governor Tim Walz, who is a middle-aged lesbian's idea of a man who will appeal to men. (I'll explain this in more detail later, but put a pin in this analysis now and know that I'm coming back to it.)

OK, who is bro group four, then? The sports bro. Some sports bros are actual athletes who have emerged from YouTube and hence overlap with the YouTube bros—Jake and Logan Paul, for instance—but the general sports bro is someone like me at OutKick or Dave Portnoy at Barstool Sports, people who made a living online in the sports universe but have since moved into pop culture and politics through the prism of sports. Now I'm admittedly more partisan in nature than many sports bros are, but the majority of the audience I have today, and many of you reading this book right now, found me in sports, not politics. One day, if we return sanity to America, I may even go back to sports full-time. But for now, the nation has gone so insane that simply picking who I think is going to win the Super Bowl feels like turning my back on the larger national debate at play.

A sports bro like me would overlap with Ben Shapiro in our Venn diagram when it came to politics. That is, and it's important to remind everyone, the manosopheres often overlap, and that's why this entire universe of primarily online male hosts has such appeal. There's a great deal of cross-pollination in these audiences and this conversation.

Joe Rogan to a large extent is a sports bro—he's one of the faces of the UFC—who has wedded his career with our fifth bro group on the internet: comedian bro. Rogan as both sports bro and comedian bro is a connector of sorts to the guys like Theo Von and Andrew Schultz, both of whom interviewed Trump as part of their podcasts. The comedian bro, based on his desire to entertain and make everyone laugh, offers a uniquely disarming way for someone like Donald Trump to interact with their audiences.

The comedy bro talks politics but often through the prism of common sense, not direct politics. And the comedy bro overlaps with Trump because both are willing to say exactly what they think and abhor the woke universe and cancel culture.

Finally, there is a sixth bro group: the just bang chicks and get rich bro. Andrew Tate is, to me, a nihilistic version of Jordan Peterson. Whereas Peterson would encourage his followers to get married, put on a suit, and aspire to raise children as part of a nuclear family, Tate would sneer at this life goal and see it as limiting. To Tate the goal of life should be to sleep with as many women as possible and get fabulously wealthy. The overlap with Elon Musk here and, frankly, many wealthy men overall, is that the nuclear family is inherently limiting in his view—the entire purpose of success is to embrace excess with women and money. Fatherhood, at least so far, is of no interest to Tate. (A prediction: Twenty years from now Tate will be extolling the importance of fatherhood as his life path evolves. But that's a prediction and not the present reality.)

Now to be fair to Tate, this is one interpretation of his bombastic worldview. When I asked my middle son, who likes some of the videos he's seen of Andrew Tate, what lessons he takes from him, he told me, "Stop whining and do more push-ups."

Which is, to be fair, not awful life advice for a young man.

I bring this up because Tate, who has faced investigations into his behavior with women all over the world, is a controversial figure, but my son's reaction to him is actually an important point here. Young men aren't necessarily embracing any one of these individuals' entire life advice guidelines or narrative arcs; they're sampling all of them due to the cross-pollinating nature of the manosphere. Sometimes that means that many men are actually sampling people with very divergent overall life philosophies because even people like Jordan Peterson and Andrew Tate would overlap in some places. Both Tate and Peterson would encourage young men to be physically active and engage in competition, for instance, seeing it as good for the development of the body, mind, and spirit.

Something that, by the way, the ancient Greeks and Romans also believed. The examination of what it means to be a man and what men should aspire to is not, ultimately, a new pursuit. It's just that only in the past twenty or so years have we begun to attack so much of conventional wisdom when it comes to traditional gender roles that much of modern manosophere thought wouldn't have been alien to say, Marcus Aurelius, the stoic Roman emperor.

OK, I'm not promising that I just gave you an exhaustive worldview here of the online manosphere, but I would guarantee you that if you have a teenage son or grandson, he has spent time online in several of these different bro-dom's I have just described.

And what is the overarching theme that all six of these universes would embrace? *That being a man is a good thing, and there is no reason to apologize for being male.*

Masculine energy is good.

It's OK, laudable even, to be a man.

I think sometimes the appeal of this message gets lost because if you're my age or older, you weren't really raised in a girl-power era. We were raised in the gender-positivity era, where it was good to be a man and also good to be a woman, but I don't remember anyone ever trying to tell me that men and women were the same or that it wasn't OK to be male, far from it.

There's a big difference between everyone should be treated equally and everyone is equal. The first is an important goal; the second is a lie. We are all very different, especially when it comes to gender.

And it's important to note that it's not just men who are responding to the manosphere. So are many women, moms, and grandmas in particular. Women don't want weak men. And many women have grown tired of the girlboss era. What it seems designed to create is an androgynous sameness. Women have been told to be more masculine, and men have been told to be more feminine. The result? Lots of women and men can't find partners, because most women don't want effeminate, wimpy men, and most men don't want masculine women.

I don't think we can discount the rise of the manosphere as a response to the #metoo era either. Starting in about 2017, many powerful men began to be held accountable for alleged inappropriate activities with women. Harvey Weinstein, the left-wing

Hollywood producer, became the face of #metoo in many respects for his alleged abuse of women. But there ended up being hundreds of targets during the era. Some were deservedly held accountable for their crimes, but many innocent men also were caught up in the era, often being accused of things they didn't do and judged guilty in the court of public opinion, despite having done nothing wrong.

Any man who attempted to speak out and acknowledge, as the actor Matt Damon did, for instance, that there was a difference between grabbing someone's butt and rape was immediately shouted down. And the #metoo era culminated in explosive Supreme Court hearings for Brett Kavanaugh, where he was accused of groping a woman at a high school party without her consent.

The accuser couldn't tell you what year the event happened or even where it happened, but the nation was transfixed by the story and the resulting Senate Supreme Court hearings. Very quickly it became a mantra of truth that if a woman alleged it happened, it happened. There was no questioning allowed. The hashtag #believeallwomen was the clarion call. Gender was truth; truth was gender. All women were saints; all men were sinners.

Is it any wonder that with masculinity itself under attack and gender weaponized to such an extent that all women were presumed to be telling the truth when they made accusations against men that there would be a backlash? And that, significantly, that backlash would grow to include not just white boys but also black, Asian, and Hispanic boys too?

Because while the white male may have initially been the target, white men are only 30 percent of the country. Eventually the target had to expand, and black, Hispanic, and Asian men found themselves under attack too.

All of this was happening at an important time in media too. Look at the six segments of the manosphere. What do they all have in common? None of them are the products of conventional big media companies. Every one emerged from the muck of the internet.

That's because the internet at its best isn't defined by top-down success, which almost never works, in fact. It thrives on bottom-up success. Rarely does great innovation online come from big companies; it mostly comes from the upstarts, the challengers, the people with nothing at all to lose. And that, interestingly enough, is exactly what I was in 2004, when I started my media career in a law office in the US Virgin Islands. While I can't speak for how all these men rose from the muck of the internet, I can tell you how I built my career online. And I think it's instructive to consider in light of the rise of the manosphere, which is really just a story about internet audio and video conquering the mainstream, legacy media. A story of the upstart disrupting the existing ecosystem. A metaphor, honestly, that isn't dissimilar for the political career of Donald Trump. But, first, how did the manosphere emerge from the internet and why have its adherents been so successful? It's because in order to win on the internet, you have to build from the bottom up, the exact opposite of the top-down process used to create media audiences.

I decided to start writing online because I had a quarter-life crisis. At the time I had an audience, legitimately, of zero people. No one had ever read anything by me online or had any idea I existed. I was twenty-five years old. I didn't even have the internet at my house. I didn't have the internet on my phone. I couldn't even send a text message, because the technology to send a text message didn't exist yet for most phones.

By 2025, OutKick, a site I hadn't even dreamed of yet, would be the most influential sports and political culture website in the country, producing an audience of tens of millions every day via web, video, and social media. I'd be hosting the largest radio show in the country, alongside Buck Sexton, and talking to over ten million people every week there, and I'd be appearing daily on Fox News, the biggest television station in the country. Altogether, it's possible I talk to more people on a daily basis on radio, the internet, and TV than, potentially, anyone in media in the United States.

How did that happen? How did I go from an audience of zero to an audience of millions?

I won on the internet.

Which is the ultimate meritocracy in media.

Let's return to that Virgin Islands law office back in 2004. It's a small office in the corner of a relatively small building. There are no pictures on the walls. There's a window looking out over Charlotte Amalie harbor, where every day large cruise ships anchor and send thousands of tourists coursing over the island when the sun comes up. Most of those people scurry back to depart by the evenings. During the day traffic piles up on the sun-dappled hills, but in the evenings, by the time I head home, the roads are mostly quiet.

If you had to pick a location under the United States flag that was less likely to produce a media company that would become the most influential in online sports, it might well be the US Virgin Islands. Only a hundred thousand people live on the three Caribbean islands that make up the USVI, and they are thousands of miles away from the continental mainland. There are no sports of particular significance played here. Other than when hurricanes hit, the mainland news pays the islands almost no attention. If you wanted to cover a big game in any sport, you would have to fly four hours to the mainland to make it happen.

There may not have been a place under the US flag less newsworthy than the USVI.

But here was my thought as I began writing online for an audience of zero. I saw the internet for what it was, a place where there were virtually no distribution costs and no editors to constrain what I said. The internet in 2004 was almost a complete meritocracy. There were very few big audience hubs, and most people who wanted to write were still clamoring to be hired by newspapers or magazines.

Everyone still wanted to be in print media.

The reason I started writing online was because no one would publish anything I wrote in print media. In fact, that summer I'd offered to provide my articles for free to the *Nashville Tennessean*, my local hometown newspaper. Their editors declined my offer of free content, saying they had no space to feature anything I produced. So writing *for free* for my hometown newspaper wasn't even an option for me. So a few friends and I built a website, and we started writing online. The goal was to entertain ourselves and, hopefully, others too. Early in those online days, back in 2004, I would dream of having a hundred readers one day; a thousand readers was a pipedream. We had a small site tracker in the right-hand corner of the site that would register each unique visitor.

Every day I would check that counter.

It grew very slowly.

But it was growing.

And every day I wrote.

I discovered something interesting about myself those first couple of years. I would show up and write every day no matter what the audience was or what the feedback was. Most people wouldn't do that. And over time I discovered something else. I was pretty good at entertaining people with words.

And here was something else I knew: Most people were bored at work and looking for a few minutes of escape, something to distract them from the work they were doing on their computers. My initial audience was young lawyers, chained to their desks, surfing the internet for something to help the day pass.

Some of you reading this book right now have been readers since back in 2004. You've been reading me for over twenty years now. I've gone from a twenty-five-year-old newlywed in the United States Virgin Islands to a forty-six-year-old father of three, who will have a college kid next fall. But all the while, beginning with an audience of zero, I was learning how the internet worked, and over time I learned the most important lesson of all: When you start with nothing, the people who become your fans on the internet will stick with you. That's because they grow with you. They take ownership in your climb because they see it as their own.

Do you know how rockstars and religions are made? Via diehard fans who become evangelists. The internet works the same way. And the internet works in the exact opposite way as the media ecosystem that had existed for generations. When I started in 2004, big media companies could make stars by putting people on television or on the radio.

As I write this in 2025, they mostly can't. The only places in media that can still mint stars are the front page of Netflix and Fox News. Everyone else is looking for stars on the internet.

The top-down media environment—big executives make stars by putting people who are unknown on TV—is over. Now almost everything comes from the bottom up. And do you know what works on the internet? I do. Because I hammer it home to my OutKick audience every single day: Smart, original, funny, and authentic content works.

If you have all four of these elements in a piece of content, it's a grand slam. If you don't have at least one of these four, it doesn't work at all.

But do you know what the most important piece of these four is? Authenticity.

Why?

Because it destroys cancel culture.

You can't cancel someone who is exactly what people think they are.

Let's pause here for one of my favorite stories. Charles Barkley, for my money the most talented sports media person in history, was arrested in Scottsdale, Arizona. It's not ideal when you're famous and you get arrested. But Barkley's arrest was a real doozy. He was arrested for driving drunk. And in the police report, Barkley apologized to the officer for driving drunk but said he was doing so because he was driving to a house because the woman there gave the best blow jobs in Arizona.

All of this is true. You can look it up.

When news broke of Barkley's DUI arrest, TNT, his employer, was astounded by the reaction. Almost no one cared. TNT took Barkley off the air for one day. And then he was back on the air. How in the world could this be the case? Because everything Charles Barkley did, right down to telling the police officer why he got the DUI, sounded exactly like something Charles Barkley would do.

Cancel culture only works when you're inauthentic.

Another story, one you're familiar with but probably haven't thought about much this way: Everyone has heard or read about the *Access Hollywood* tape, when Donald Trump told Billy Bush that when you're famous you can grab women by the pussy. This recording was supposed to be the death blow to Trump's 2016 presidential campaign. You'll recall that many Republicans even demanded that Trump drop out of the race after this tape surfaced in October of 2016.

But it turned out, people didn't really care. Why? Because Trump bragging that you should just grab women by the pussy sounded like something Trump would say. He got elected president. Cancel culture, just like with Barkley, didn't work on him.

But what happened to Billy Bush?

By then employed by the *Today Show*, Bush was fired from his TV job and his wife left him. Think about this for a moment. Trump gets elected president, and Billy Bush can't even work on TV anymore? How the hell does this happen? It's an example of bottom-up versus top-down media. Bush's bosses were embarrassed by his association with the tape and fired him. Trump's bosses, the American voters, elected him president.

The lesson: The media is mostly bullshit.

And Trump's genius is that he knew it before anyone else in politics did.

And he knew he wasn't actually being judged by the media; he was being judged by the people, who also, in the back of their minds, knew the media was bullshit too.

It's not just Trump either. Bill and Hillary Clinton also benefited from their respective brands when it came to their own scandals. Bill Clinton kept his job even though he got a blow job from an intern in the Oval Office. How in the world does that happen? That's bonkers. Maybe. But it's also, if you remember Clinton's brand, kind of predictable. Most people, deep down, weren't actually that surprised Clinton was getting a blow job from an intern. They might not have been happy about it, but it definitely seemed like something he might do.

Another media example, this one benefiting Hillary. Remember when she claimed to have been under fire in Iraq? It turned out to be completely made up. Yet she paid almost no political price for it. Meanwhile Brian Williams, then NBC's lead anchor, made up the same story about being under fire, and his career essentially ended. Why? Because Americans expected Hillary to lie, and they expected Brian Williams to tell the truth. But also because NBC, as with Billy Bush, reacted in a top-down manner: They fired Williams before we even found out whether his viewers cared about this scandal at all.

Remember my First Amendment and boobs moment? The people who knew me weren't surprised at all that I said it. The people who hated me wanted me fired. The people who didn't know me? They probably broke 70–30 as being entertained. But guess what? If I'd apologized, everyone would have hated me. Because my apology would have been bullshit.

And people hate bullshit.

Especially people on the internet, who make stars from the bottom up.

The internet rewards authenticity more than anything. As long as you stay true to the expectations of your audience, your audience never leaves you.

Somehow Trump understood this innately better than almost anyone in the history of politics. Even though Trump was from the old-media era, he understood the rules of new media better than any of the people who have run against him. And Trump was even willing to say it explicitly. Remember when he said he could shoot someone on Fifth Avenue and his audience wouldn't leave him? He wasn't wrong. Trump's audience was willing to forgive things he did that would have destroyed other politicians, because they believed in his authenticity. He wasn't perfect, but he wasn't steeped in bullshit either.

And most of media life, people came to discover, was bullshit.

Trump's political life, in many ways, is just one long gamble that people like Trump and that as long as he keeps acting like Trump, he'll be fine. This is fascinating because Trump has been a media figure for so long that he's moved from a top-down fame—he got famous on traditional TV and newspapers—and then got elected president by social media and the internet.

I've got all sorts of opinions that people disagree with vehemently. (All musicals suck. No man should play the flute. Alabama Crimson Tide fans are the dumbest in sports.) But what I've found is that the more opinionated I am, the more people like me, not because people agree with me on everything but just because they respect the fact that I say exactly what I think. I don't tiptoe up to anything. As a result, there's no opinion I can share at this point that can get me canceled.

This is the exact opposite of the way modern media is run, even now!

Let me give you an example: Don Lemon was on CNN for years. Every night for eight years, he was there on your TV screen on his own show, talking about the latest news story. Millions of people watched him every night. After years of mostly mediocre news coverage—he once asked if it was possible a black hole devoured the Malaysian Airlines missing flight—Don Lemon became an avowed Trump hater during the first Trump term.

His ratings soared.

Then Joe Biden won.

And no one paid attention to Don Lemon any longer. CNN decided to move him to mornings, where he mostly was ignored, until he decided to say Nikki Haley, then running for president in 2023, was past her prime at the age of fifty-one. When his cohosts pushed back, Lemon refused to apologize, telling them to google when a woman was in her prime.

The resulting brouhaha eventually led to Lemon being fired a few months later. Suddenly off CNN for the first time in nearly a decade, Lemon attempted to rebuild his career on the internet with a show designed to compete there. But here's the problem: No one really cares about him on the internet. And he's gone from competing with only two other channels on cable news, MSNBC and Fox News, to competing with an infinite number of voices online.

Lemon was a top-down host of limited interest to the general public. He isn't smart, original, funny, or authentic enough to win on the internet. This isn't intended to be a knock on Lemon. Most TV people don't work on the internet either. Because the internet is far more competitive than TV. On TV news you have to compete with only three channels: Fox News, MSNBC, and CNN. On the internet you have to compete with everyone. On TV sports, you have to compete with just ESPN and FS1. Skip Bayless had a substantial audience on sports TV. But on the internet? No one cares.

Some have transitioned well to the internet—Tucker Carlson, Megyn Kelly, and Piers Morgan among them—but the vast majority of TV newspeople, both sports and politics, are lost in the cavalcade of voices online.

I like to joke that those of us who have come up through the internet are tougher, more battle hardened, and far more proven than those who came top down from big media companies. We're like Bane in the Batman movies. I love the monologue when he tells Batman, "Ah, you think darkness is your ally? You merely adopted the dark. I was born in it, molded by it. I didn't see the light until I was already a man, by then it was nothing to me but blinding."

I worked on the internet for a decade before I stepped foot in a TV studio. The lights were blinding that first day in the studio, but I didn't care. I'd been living in the dark for a long time. I knew I could always go back to the internet. What did I have to lose on TV? Now you see networks scrambling to put internet stars on TV. Pat McAfee at ESPN. MrBeast on Amazon. Everyone is trying to take the stars built on the internet now and put them on TV; the world has changed, and Trump saw this before most.

A sidenote here for a moment: It's hard to be authentic. Some of you reading this right now who are interested in media careers are thinking, *OK, I'll just be authentic, then*. Most people can't do it, especially not in media. There's something about the attention and the bright lights that breaks people. Fox Sports has a green room where everyone hangs out when they aren't on-air. It's a sports fan's dream. You're sitting in front of a bank of TVs showing every NFL game with Jimmy Johnson, Michael Strahan, Howie Long, and Terry Bradshaw, or you're watching all the college football games with Matt Leinart, Joel Klatt, and Eddie George. Seriously, it's awesome.

I have seen dozens of famous people in that green room who are some of the best storytellers, the most relaxed guys and gals on the planet, people you would want to hang out with all night long, but then they walk sixty yards down the hallway to the studio, and those bright lights bear down on them, that red light goes on the camera, and they panic. They freeze up. They're a pinprick as interesting as they were before the cameras went live.

Some guys in sports are practice-player juggernauts. They look incredible when the games don't count, but as soon as the crowd and the bright lights are there and the real game arrives, they freeze up. They can't perform the same as they did in practice.

For whatever reason I'm almost the exact same on a radio microphone or in front of a camera as I am when the radio and cameras aren't on. I don't freeze up. I don't get tense. I'm just as relaxed. That doesn't mean TV or radio are easy or I don't work my ass off to prepare for both. It just means authenticity is harder than you think to pull off in a media ecosystem.

Most people can't do it.

They worry what others will think. They trip over their words. They pull their punches. They say what they think people want to hear. They aren't real.

And Trump innately, intuitively gets that too.

For better or worse, he's always Trump.

Think about this for a moment too. One of the things I learned in sports was that most college football recruits don't pay attention to anything until they're about ten years old. By the time they are getting recruited at fifteen or sixteen, this means they only have a five- or six-year window of memory. Anything that happened more than six years ago is ancient history to them. It might as well have been thirty years ago. The internet is immediate culture, not historic culture. The internet perfectly fits the brain cycle of young men; it's where they go to see the authentic, undistilled truth from people they trust.

Trump came down the escalator for the first time in 2015. My oldest son was eight years old, my middle son was five years old, and my youngest son was a year old. Trump has been a character in their entire lives. And what kind of character has he been, according to most in the legacy media? A rebel, the person no one liked, a bad guy, the person everyone blamed for everything. Trump has been *them*. He is these kids, the young boys who have come of age in an era when they are blamed for everything.

Intuitively they know that isn't true. They have no power or agency. How could they have caused anything to be wrong in the country? As these young boys have gotten older, they've come to see that they truly haven't done anything wrong, that they haven't been worthy of blame. Is it any surprise they'd see a common narrative connection to Trump?

Trump was the avatar of internet life, the bad boy bearing the brunt of blame for everything he hadn't actually done. He was their spirit animal, the ultimate bad guy who was actually a good guy.

Think about it.

Within days of January 6, 2021, Facebook, Twitter, YouTube, Spotify, Snapchat, Instagram, Shopify, Reddit, Twitch, TikTok, and Pinterest all banned Donald Trump from having accounts on their social media sites.

Pinterest!

They wouldn't even let Donald Trump share his cooking photos and his corkboard collages, the bastards!

It was a staggering censorship campaign. If all of these companies could collude to censor Donald Trump, what power does a regular person have in the internet age? Virtually none. Of course this wasn't all they would do to Trump. They would also later attempt to bankrupt and imprison him, but the censorship was about removing Trump from the public square. If Trump couldn't reach his audience and share his every thought, his power, the thinking went, would vanish.

Now the reality, of course, was that Trump would eventually start his own Truth Social account, and as I write this, that stake is worth several billion dollars to Trump, but the ultimate result of all this collusion wasn't to exclude Trump from the national conversation; it was to make him a free speech martyr.

It also revealed quite a lot about the censorious left wing. When you ban someone, you're acknowledging that their ideas are powerful in some way. You don't censor people with no power; you censor people because you fear their power. As I've said for a long time, the people who burn books are never the good guys. (Conservatives don't "ban" books, by the way. They argue about what books are age appropriate to have in libraries. An R-rated movie isn't "banned." It's just restricted by age. If local news can't show all the pages of a book, call me crazy, but it shouldn't be in an elementary school library.)

When you censor a politician, it's almost always the case that you fear the power of his ideas. What was seen in January of 2021 as a strength of the left wing's ascension to power, the banning of Trump, became the seeds of their own undoing because it made left-wing ideas flabby, untested, and out of shape. When you control the social media algorithms and rig the debate in your favor, you don't strengthen your own side's arguments. You weaken them. Every Republican with even a modicum of activity online is immersed in left-wing arguments, but almost no Democrat was aware of right-wing arguments. When the referee is always on your side—and the social media referees were always on the Democrat side, make no mistake about it—you don't develop strong arguments of your own; you get used to a scoreboard where you start off several touchdowns ahead.

And you aren't prepared for a real fight online.

What was seen in 2021 as a cultural strength of the left—their cancellation of their chief adversary, Donald Trump—would become, as 2024 moved closer, a Pyrrhic victory. Left-wingers had won the battle against Trump online, but it appeared they might be losing the war, particularly when you saw how much young men were gravitating toward banned Trump content online. Throughout history the young have flocked to that which they aren't supposed to see.

When I was a kid, it was *Playboy* magazines, but for today's young men, it was Donald Trump and right-wing ideas.

From January 6, 2021, to November 5, 2024, was less than four years, but it was also the greatest political comeback of all time. And it was uniquely rooted in the internet ecosystem. Trump remade himself from the ground up. His rise back to power wasn't a top-down affair. Heck, even Fox News banned him. The *New York Post* buried his reelection announcement in the print newspaper. Trump was left in the media wilderness. He rose through the back channels of the internet, from the ground up, like every star of the internet has always conquered more traditional, legacy media.

What happened in 2024 wasn't just that young men moved toward Trump. It was that the social media algorithms and guardrails suddenly collapsed, providing an even playing field all of a sudden. And as the walls came crumbling down that protected the big media castles, the upstart rebels of the internet and the companies they've founded became the new kings of media.

The Trump 2024 campaign reminds me of the videos you sometimes see of people at zoos taunting tigers behind the glass. Generally, you can get away with this, but every so often the glass shatters, and you aren't protected from the tigers any more. It happened at the San Francisco Zoo on Christmas Day in 2007.

Several men taunted a tiger. Later investigations uncovered that the wall keeping the tiger in the enclosure was several feet too low, but no one knew because the tiger had never attempted to climb the wall because he hadn't been antagonized like that before. One man was killed near the tiger enclosure; two others were mauled. It took zoo officials a long time to respond because they didn't believe it was possible the tiger could escape his cage.

But do a Google search, and it turns out this happens quite often. Many people taunt wild animals, confident the cages keep them safe.

But every now and then the animals escape.

Democrats thought they had Trump caged.

They were wrong.

And when Trump was unleashed, there was hell to pay.

I'm going to explain all of this in detail—the great collapse of legacy media and how it coincided with Trump's big 2024 win— but I love this metaphor, which sometimes becomes reality. There's a big difference between a tiger in a cage and a tiger outside of a cage. Everything changes in an instant.

We'll come back to the tiger metaphor and how it intersects with the collapse of the internet, but for now let's return to the banning of Trump. When every major media company on the internet works in concert to ban someone, it's the definition of a top-down decision. No company CEO was unaware of the choice being made. You don't ban the sitting president of the United States from your platform without the company leaders being involved.

They all knew they were banning Trump.

But what they didn't know was that they were creating a new Trump, one connecting with the same young men society was trying to ban. And these young men came to see him as their champion as a result. What's more rebellious than supporting someone banned on the internet? Many of the books being written about the 2024 campaign, I think, have made it appear that Trump won because he connected with young men. I think that's wrong. I think young men connected with Trump and then Trump, intuitive showman that he is, felt their energy and reflected their support.

I'll share some stories later in the book about my own interactions with Trump, but one of Trump's best attributes is he gets media better than most of the people in media. He could have, and maybe should have, been a media executive himself.

And the biggest difference of Trump's 2016 campaign to his 2024 campaign was this: The legacy media was collapsing, the top-down media apparatus was losing almost all of its power, and everything was coming from the internet now. Trump's own authenticity destroyed the lack of authenticity from the legacy media. His very existence served as a taunt to all of them, which is why one of the great untold stories of the Trump era so far is that Trump's overall approval ratings have grown during his political tenure, while the legacy media's have cratered to all-time lows.

Think about this for a minute: In trying to destroy Trump, the legacy media has actually destroyed themselves instead.

OK, some of you may be wondering, *What do you mean by the legacy media?* The answer is pretty simple: CNN, MSNBC, *The New York Times*, *The Washington Post*, CBS, NBC, ABC. Basically, if you made opposing Trump your mission when he was elected and banked massive amounts of subscription or advertising revenue predicated on attacking his awfulness and lack of fitness for office, you're who I'm talking about.

All of these legacy media business models collapsed as soon as Joe Biden was elected in 2020—he was awful for their businesses— but something interesting happened as Trump began his political comeback: The subscribers didn't return. There was no new surge in subscriptions. The ratings didn't soar at MSNBC or at CNN. *The New York Times* and *The Washington Post* didn't have a glut of new subscribers. Trump, the great Satan of the left, was back, stronger than ever, Adolf Hitler reborn anew, yet the legacy media couldn't corral an audience. The business model wasn't working. What the heck was going on?

I was pretty sure I knew, and I was saying it all throughout the rise of Trump 2.0. Trump was imperfect and flawed like all of us, but he wasn't as awful as the caricature espoused by Kamala Harris and Joe Biden. He wasn't Hitler, not even close. He was authentically Trump.

And once the general public decides who you are, what's done to you becomes secondary to their opinion of you. You can raid Mar-a-Lago, you can arrest and mugshot him, you can put him on trial for months in New York City for sex with a pornstar, you can try to bankrupt him with sexual assault trials in civil court, but what you can't do is change the public's opinion of Trump.

As the 2024 campaign progressed and Joe Biden floundered in his Trump attacks, an ominous sign began to arise: Democrat ads ripping Trump for his arrest and his mugshot weren't having the desired effect. In fact, they were doing something extraordinary: They were actually lifting Trump in the polls and increasing his favorability ratings.

How in the world could this be happening?

Simple. Everything Trump was accused of sounded like something Trump might have done. And just like Bill Clinton when he was impeached over the Monica Lewinsky scandal, when you try to punish someone too much for something the public thinks they are likely to have done, it actually starts to look like a rig job.

Trump, brilliantly, saw all of this coming.

Which is why he leaned into the persecution.

He made his mugshot into T-shirts and sold them to raise money for his presidential candidacy. Young men loved it because they knew it was all bullshit. And, finally, someone else was saying what they innately knew to be true.

At Mar-a-Lago during a commercial break in one of our radio interviews, Trump gestured frenetically to his aide Margo. "Go get the T-shirts," he told her. "I have to sign them for the boys," he said, meaning Buck and me.

During another commercial break, he stood over the T-shirt, large black magic marker in his hand, as he signed them with a flourish. He was like Leonardo da Vinci stepping back to admire the Mona Lisa.

"You know," he said, "I was hoping it [the mugshot] would look good, but I never thought it could look this great."

He smiled at us.

"Can you believe it?" he asked with his trademark Trump smirk. "What a load of bullshit."

CHAPTER 7

Trump in Full

I T WAS EARLY IN THE MORNING ON AUGUST 11, 2020, and the phone was ringing in our Fox Sports Radio studios. I was back home in my Nashville studio, and my producer Danny G. picked up the phone out in our Los Angeles studio. On the other end was President Donald Trump, calling for an interview on my sports talk radio show.

Later, after the interview was over, Danny G. and I would talk about how the interview went, but Danny G. would marvel over one thing: Trump called himself. When he picked up the ringing phone in our studio, Trump was on the other end, and he had a casual conversation with my producer. It blew Danny G. away because even most pro athletes don't call a sports talk show. They have their public relations person call and patch them through, yet here was Trump, the actual president of the United States, calling a few minutes early to chat with my producer. (In typical Trump fashion, he would tell my producer he deserved a raise.)

Many people want to know how you end up interviewing the president of the United States, and the simple answer is this: The president, or his staff, decides he wants to talk with you. That's how my first Trump interview happened. One day my phone rang from a blocked number, I picked it up, and the White House was calling to ask if I'd like to have President Trump on my radio show.

I'm not going to lie, that's a nice call to get.

Especially since I'd been saying for years that Trump was going to come on my OutKick the Coverage sports talk radio show, and no one had believed me. In fact, everyone had mocked the idea, including my own family.

But it made total logical sense to me.

And reaching out to us on my sports talk radio show in 2020 was actually an early version of the 2024 campaign. Trump wanted to reach nontraditional audiences with his message, especially persuadable men. He knew my audience was filled with diehard sports fans who would also, likely, be open to hearing from him. Sure, he could do another interview with a news channel, but in doing so he'd likely be talking to the same audience all over again. Why not broaden his outreach and speak to sports fans, especially since Trump himself was a big sports fan?

I have zero doubt that a sports fan, Trump, talking to other sports fans back in 2020 likely increased his overall vote total. By how much? I have no idea. No one does, but remember that Trump increased his 2020 vote total by over 11 million votes, from 62.9 million votes in 2016 to 74.2 million votes in 2020. The 2024 campaign took that number to 77.3 million Trump votes, but the biggest growth in Trump support actually happened from 2016 to 2020 and that campaign, to a large extent, set the template for the outright popular vote win in 2024. (As an aside, this book isn't designed to relitigate the 2020 election, but Joe Biden's 81.3 million votes in 2020 is staggering to see compared to the Democratic vote totals in 2008, 2012, 2016, and 2024. Consider: Barack Obama got 69.5 million votes in 2008 and 65.9 million votes in 2012. Hillary Clinton got 65.8 million votes in 2016, nearly identical to Obama in 2012, and then Joe Biden got 81.3 million votes in 2020?! Only to see Kamala drop back down to 75 million in 2024. Which one of these looks like a crazy outlier? Biden's 2020 voting tally, now that we've seen Trump run three times so we can compare how many votes he banks for himself and motivates for the other side, look, frankly, unbelievable. It's like the home run numbers during the steroids era in baseball; something just isn't adding up.)

I have interviewed Trump now eleven different times, in person in New Jersey, Florida, Washington, DC, and Alabama, and on the phone several times too. In total, I have interviewed him for six or seven hours, probably more than almost anyone in media anywhere in the world, both solo and with my radio show cohost Buck Sexton.

In the previous chapter, I talked about Trump's great skill, his authenticity. In this chapter, I want to explain to you what that looks like and how it translates on radio and TV via stories surrounding those interviews, not the interviews themselves, necessarily, but the surrounding environments. The kinds of things a writer might notice that don't translate themselves into the actual words and answers given in an interview but that help to explain how Trump, uniquely, saw and exploited the rapidly shifting media environment from 2015 to the 2024 election.

What makes, in other words, Trump Trump and how did that work to create his electoral landslide in 2024?

That first interview call, where Trump called himself, is a good example. He casually chatted with our producer and then during the course of our conversation on live sports talk radio never appeared rushed at all. Every time I've interviewed Trump, I've gotten the sense there's nothing else he'd rather be doing. He has an incredible ability to be present in the moment.

The second time I interviewed Trump, he was late. It was just a month or so later, and he was coming on my radio show again. Only he hadn't called in, and no one else would make the phone call on his staff but him. After I texted a couple of White House aides, they tracked him down, and he called my producer. Yet again he told Danny G. that he deserved a raise and talked with him on the phone in casual chitchat as he waited for a commercial break to end and our interview to begin.

It often feels like many politicians are trying to figure out what you want and then give it back to you. There's a desperation to it, a cloying nature. It's actually the opposite of leadership. It's just following your lead and trying to make you think they've been a few steps ahead of you the entire time. Trump doesn't do that; he's just Trump.

That creates its own challenges. Trump says and does things that are total messes for him and actually makes his job more difficult, but the mess he creates, ironically, endears him to his audience because that mess is so apolitical. That is, the bull in a China shop analogy, which is accurate, ultimately works in Trump's favor. How many times have you heard someone in the legacy media pronounce Trump's latest antics as disqualifying? Yet they never are. Why? Because Trump's authenticity protects him. As I said in an earlier chapter, authenticity cancels cancel culture.

While I had interviewed him twice on the radio, I still had never met President Trump in person. The first time I met him in person was in the Oval Office in October of 2020, just a couple of weeks before the election. Trump did an interview with OutKick's Jason Whitlock, but the White House team invited me to bring my wife and my oldest son, who was in seventh grade, to make the trip too. The Trump team had offered for all the kids to be there, but my wife was terrified, probably accurately, that my boys would get in a fight in the White House, and she'd spend the entire visit trying to separate them from each other. So we only had our oldest son.

Likely, at the time, prepped by his staff, Trump swept out onto the walkway outside the Oval Office, where the OutKick interview was set up. He saw me, said hello to me by name, and said he loved OutKick. Then he sat down and started the interview.

I've got to confess that the president of the United States greeting you by name is a pretty incredible feeling. Trump, as I've come to find out, is fantastic at giving shout-outs to supporters during his speeches. You've probably seen this happen on television. It's a boring part of the address for most people, and the TV networks often cut away from it, but it's invaluable in building support and bona fides. And Trump, I learned that day for the first time, is exceptional at it.

Immediately after the OutKick interview, President Trump came into the Oval Office, where my wife and son had been ushered in for the meeting. Trump spent at least ten minutes with my son in particular. He peppered him with White House factoids, gave him an old wooden key that's supposed to be a replica of the key they used for the White House hundreds of years ago, signed a red MAGA hat for him, and posed for photos alongside all of us in the Oval Office. My wife, like many college-educated women, wasn't a huge fan of Trump before she met him. Afterward, she couldn't stop talking about how nice he was. (He added a vote that day: hers, based entirely on how he treated my son and our family.)

To this day, when anyone asks what Trump is like, my wife reverts to this description of him: He's an incredibly nice guy. He asks questions of you, listens to your answers, and engages. For someone who is a superstar, and has been for decades, Trump wears his fame lightly. He's comfortable in his own skin, a born showman, and he genuinely likes people and enjoys spending time with them.

The next time I interviewed Trump in person was at Mar-a-Lago in February of 2022, just as the Russia invasion of Ukraine was occurring. Buck and I did the entire radio show from the Mar-a-Lago ballroom, and Trump came on with us for a full hour that day. Usually politicians are surrounded by staffers and there's abundant discussions about topics and which questions are going to be asked. Not with Trump. He came in with only one aide, Margo Martin, who has spent the past several years delivering amazing behind-the-scenes videos of the Trump campaign and now the Trump White House—and told us to ask him anything.

After the first commercial break, he leaned back and said, "This is fantastic. I feel like I'm in therapy. I get to talk about everything I've been wanting to talk about." (Trump has long been a fan of live radio because, unlike many interviews, it can't be edited to change what he says.) At the time of that interview, Trump's opportunities to speak to large audiences had been drastically curtailed because Fox News was in the middle of a lawsuit about the 2020 election and wasn't allowing him on the airwaves, certainly not live.

We asked him whether he would be running in 2024, and Trump declined to answer, but during the commercial break, after the questions, he took his headset off, leaned back in his chair, and said he thought we'd like his answer. The difference between Trump on-air and Trump during commercial breaks, by the way, is nonexistent. He's the exact same person at all times. His authenticity is both his political sword and shield.

Our interview made major international news that day, but Trump was thrilled with the entire experience. That summer we broadcast our Clay and Buck radio show from Bedminster, New Jersey, where Trump was hosting the LIV golf tournament on his golf course there. (I played one of the most disastrous pro-am rounds in the history of Bedminster the previous day. In fact, I narrowly avoided drilling my playing partner, Brooks Koepka, with an errant iron shot.) We broadcast from a family cottage there on the property for another hour. Trump sat at the table in a polo shirt, a red MAGA hat, and golf slacks, pounding Diet Cokes and talking golf during every commercial break.

This time accompanied by his aide Taylor Budowich, Trump sat down at the table, told us to ask anything, and even bullshitted some about my golf game. "I heard you were crushing the ball all over the course," he said. Nothing could be further from the truth. In fact Greg Norman, head of LIV Golf at the time, had said the previous day, "You have a nice golf swing. Looks like my grandma's. Of course, she's been dead for ages."

During one of our commercial breaks, Donald Trump Jr. and his children came in to visit, including Kai, his granddaughter, a talented high school golfer at the time who has since committed to play women's golf at the University of Miami. Immediately Trump turned into a grandpa. He asked if Kai had brought her clubs and wanted to play with him that afternoon. Trump as grandpa is a side of him that doesn't get seen very often, but they did a much better job of showing that in the 2024 campaign.

You would never have known Trump was a president then. For all the world, he was just a grandpa wanting to hear how his grandkids were doing. Indeed, the more time you spend around Trump, what becomes clear is the caricature of him as an authoritarian dictator, a Hitler-like evil leader with awful intentions, is just not true at all. In fact, I think there's a strong argument that Trump is the most unfairly treated politician of any of our lives.

It's not just that the legacy media gets many stories about him wrong; it's that they never get any stories about him wrong that benefit him. That is, if the media was just negligent, there would be many stories in *The New York Times*, *The Washington Post*, CBS, NBC, and ABC that were inaccurate but made Trump look better than he otherwise would. Yet, think about it. Can you even come up with a single one of these stories?

I can't.

That spring of 2023, we traveled to Mar-a-Lago for a fundraiser for Senator Bill Hagerty of Tennessee, and Trump came to speak to the attendees. There were probably fifty or so of us, and Trump addressed the group from the back patio overlooking his pool. On multiple occasions he referred to me by name and the important work I was doing on the radio show. My wife, meeting Trump for the second time, was even more impressed at his kindness and showmanship.

At seventy-seven years old, somehow Trump was possessed with an unending fountain of youth, energy that most men and women decades younger didn't have.

Back home in Nashville in the summer of 2023, Trump came to do a fundraiser, and their campaign team invited me to come visit with him. I brought my two youngest boys with me this time for their first meeting with Trump. A long line of greeters stood waiting for their moment with the president, who was there standing for hours posing for photos and interacting with all the visitors.

He was fabulous with both my kids, grilling my middle son, who had hit his first Little League home run earlier that day, about baseball, and kidding with my youngest son about what it was like to have two older brothers. And it wasn't just with us. The line to meet his supporters stretched on for hours. Then would come a dinner and a speech. And this was just a single trip to Nashville. He was doing this to raise money all over the country. For every person there, it was a moment they'd remember forever. For him, it was an act he'd do ten thousand times or more.

Yet somehow he kept his energy up and performed for the entire crowd.

Not for the first time, I thought it was extraordinary.

During the 2024 campaign, in November of 2023, we traveled to Mar-a-Lago again for the Clay and Buck radio show, and Trump walked right in for his interview with us from playing eighteen holes, still in his golf spikes and his golfing attire and did a full hour with us from one of the reception rooms inside his private club. Once again there was no prep, no discussion about topics. Trump sat down, put his headset on, and started answering questions.

As I mentioned earlier in the book, he signed T-shirts of his mugshot for us then.

But also Buck and I had our wives with us for that interview. Buck and his wife, Carrie, lived in Miami, and we were driving back to Miami from Palm Beach, Florida, after the interview. Trump refused to allow us to leave until we'd all four gotten milkshakes. "We make the best milkshakes in the country here," Trump said in typical Trump understatement.

So we all waited around for our milkshakes, which were, to be fair, fabulous.

I remember joking as we drank our milkshakes that Hitler was, of course, renowned for insisting that his guests stick around for the world-famous milkshakes in his club kitchen.

On July 12, 2024, Trump came on the Clay and Buck show and teed off on two Olympics boxers with XY chromosomes—that is, biological males—being allowed to win women's gold medals. In addition to the news he made with that opinion, it nearly was the final interview Trump would do in his life. The shooting in Butler, Pennsylvania, would occur the next day.

Finally, during the final weeks of the 2024 campaign, we did an interview inside his stadium suite at the Georgia-Alabama football game on September 28, 2024, just a few weeks before the election. And let me set the scene for you.

For those of you who are not college football fans, Georgia and Alabama have been the two best teams in the Southeastern Conference for much of the past six or seven years. Georgia was 3–0 and ranked number two in the nation, and Alabama was 3–0 and ranked number four in the nation. It was the first major game for new Alabama coach Kalen DeBoer, taking over for the legendary Nick Saban, and all of Tuscaloosa was completely electric in the days leading up to the game.

In my always humble opinion, there is no better place to be in the country than in the South for a major college football game. I wrote my first book, *Dixieland Delight*, about the pomp, circumstance, and pageantry of a fall Saturday in the South, but on this day, given the opponents and the president coming to the game, it was absolutely electric.

I had my fourteen-year-old son with me—who is fantastic but for the fact that he's elected to become an Alabama fan, a decision that has frequently left me apoplectic—and I'd done television hits for Fox News and Fox Sports's Big Noon Kickoff pregame show that morning. The debate between Trump and Kamala had been just a few weeks earlier, and Alabama fans wore lapel pins that said, "They're eating the Dawgs," a reference to Trump's comments that illegal immigrants were eating house pets in Ohio. Several fraternities draped banners outside their houses that levied the most divisive insult of all: "Georgia fans are voting for Kamala."

On fraternity row OutKick's Caity McDuffie took Trump and Kamala baseball hats and had students pick who they were voting for via hat ceremonies, a knockoff of how top recruits often announce their school picks. The Alabama students staged elaborate hat choices, tossing the Kamala hat to the side and endorsing Trump by placing the MAGA hats on their heads in celebratory fashion. Every single Alabama fraternity member she spoke with was voting for Trump, an early sign, one that I'd seen repeated all over the South, of Trump's strength with college-aged male voters.

What's more, when we posted the videos on OutKick's social media accounts, they went immediately viral, spreading across TikTok, Twitter, Instagram, and beyond. In 2016, and even in 2020, many young people who voted for Trump felt compelled to hide their support. No longer. As I watched young people sharing our videos widely, I remarked to my fourteen-year-old that I was astounded by how many people appeared to be voting Trump in Tuscaloosa.

"Dad," he told me, "almost every kid in my school would vote Trump if we could." (The kids in his school would later vote 80–20 for Trump in their in-house school election, but the faculty, interestingly, voted 75–25. The culture and vibe shift was very real with young men in particular. I could feel and see it.)

With Trump scheduled to arrive in Tuscaloosa, it was bedlam everywhere in the streets, so I took my fourteen-year-old back to our hotel, and we did what any father and son wants to do on a big college football weekend—we watched games. The previous night we had stayed up late to watch Miami avoid a last-second loss to Virginia Tech after a Hokie Hail Mary catch that was initially ruled a touchdown was overruled. (Sorry, Hokie fans, I still don't understand how that call was overturned either.) Now we watched games and counted down the hours until we'd be back in the stadium.

As we watched Kentucky play at Ole Miss, I jotted down potential questions for Trump, knowing it would be a chaotic scene in the stadium suite and that I'd only have around ten minutes to get the entire interview complete. The previous day our OutKick video staff, Charles and Ryan, had traveled with our gear to get it set up in the suite, but I still hadn't had a chance to test our audio or do a dry run. We'd be conducting the only interview of Trump that day, and we'd be doing it without a safety net.

It's probably not a surprise that all three of my boys have become huge college football fans as I've done my best to bring them on the road for big games as often as I can. Indeed, on our drive to Tuscaloosa on the prior day, my son and I talked about the best college football game he says he'd ever seen in person, the legendary game between LSU and Alabama in November of 2019. Trump had also attended that game, which ended in a thrilling 46–41 victory for Joe Burrow's LSU Tigers. Burrow, who ended an eight-game Alabama winning streak in the rivalry, threw for 393 yards and three touchdowns and outdueled Alabama's Tua Tagovailoa in the process.

On that day in October of 2019, President Trump had been in a suite waving out at a cheering crowd. I took video from the stands. As we watched games that afternoon, I looked up those videos and showed them to my son. He'd been nine years old then. Now he was fourteen. It was amazing to see how much he'd grown. "You know," he said as we looked at the videos and pictures from that game, "I'll be able to vote in the next presidential election."

My jaw dropped.

I know it's a cliché, but your kids go from Little League age to adults in the blink of an eye. I can't believe that in 2028 I'll have two adult sons. But I'm so glad for the sporting events we've been able to attend together.

After that LSU win back in 2019, feeling bad for my nine-year-old Bama fan son, I asked him how he wanted to spend the rest of the night, and he said he wanted to get chicken tenders from Bojangles and Taco Bell tacos and watch more college football games in the hotel. Now, five years later, he didn't care at all about my scheduled interview with Trump. He just wanted to watch the game.

"Are you sure the interview will be over before the game starts?" he asked.

"Yes," I said, "that's the plan."

Given the recent two assassination attempts, security was ratcheted up to an incredible level for the game, making it much more difficult to get inside the stadium than for an ordinary game. (Just like in 2019, fans were advised to arrive at least an hour before kickoff.) Every fan arriving for the game had to go through the normal metal detectors and then a secondary level of metal detectors too. We were scheduled to interview Trump just before kickoff and supposed to meet the Secret Service agents to be security wanded and cleared before the game. But word arrived from his staff that Trump would be running late. So we started off the game in our seats.

Then, just as kickoff arrived, came word that Trump would be arriving sooner than expected, so we were rushed across the stadium to the suite where Trump would be. Usually the suites in

Alabama's stadium have several rows outdoors to allow fans to go inside and outside for the game, but those seats had been blocked in the Trump suite in favor of newly installed bulletproof shields, which were placed outside and blocked anyone from sitting in the outdoor seats.

Inside the suite a motley crew of famous Trump supporters were gathered awaiting the arrival of the president: Kid Rock, Hank Williams Jr., the golfer John Daly, Georgia Bulldog legend Herschel Walker, the UFC fighter Colby Covington, Senators Katie Britt, Tommy Tuberville, Steve Daines, and more all crowded into a suite designed for twenty people that probably featured a hundred or more constantly rotating through.

Trump wasn't even there yet, but the combination of a huge football game and the arrival of Trump had the suite bouncing with energy. And it was hot, very hot. The suite's air conditioning couldn't keep pace with the crowd inside and the outdoor heat. As we stood there, word arrived that the interview would be pushed to halftime as Trump still hadn't arrived midway through the first quarter.

My fourteen-year-old son, wearing a Jalen Milroe Alabama quarterback jersey, groaned.

Given a choice between meeting Trump or having Alabama win the football game, he'd pick Alabama winning, and it wasn't a close call at all.

Luckily for him, Alabama was off to a fast start, surging out to a 21–0 lead as Georgia's defense had no answer for Jalen Milroe.

Suddenly, Trump arrived in the stadium.

Immediately social media lit up with footage of him in the bowels of Bryant-Denny Stadium. He'd purchased boxes of chicken tenders and was throwing them to fans. The entire vibe on the suite level where I was shifted. Fans walking by craned their necks to try to catch a glimpse of Trump and the celebrities flocking to see him. In particular, young, college-aged students and recent grads swarmed the area. Later their videos would ricochet across Tik-Tok, Instagram reels, and YouTube.

This was very different from what had happened in 2019 inside the stadium. Then, the older Alabama fans had seemed the most excited to see Trump. This was a youth movement. It felt more like Trump was a music celebrity than a politician. It reminded me, frankly, of how Taylor Swift's fans reacted when she was in their presence in a stadium, either for her own performance or to watch Travis Kelce play a Kansas City Chiefs football game.

As Caity McDuffee showed me the viral numbers on her hat selection videos from the frat houses, it was clear that something was happening, a movement, much different from 2016 or 2020, was building online. Young people were connecting with Trump in a way they never had before.

Heck, even the videos of Trump tossing chicken tender baskets in the recesses of the stadium were going viral and getting tens of millions of views.

As we waited to interview Trump, I showed my fourteen-year-old the videos going viral of Trump inside the stadium. "Everybody loves him," he said. "Everybody."

"Why?" I asked.

"People love his TikToks, his "YMCA" dancing. He's like everybody's favorite grandpa." (Shortly after Trump was elected, my fourteen-year-old texted me, "Dad, you won't believe it. Trump just saved TikTok!")

We were all standing now just outside Trump's suite. At any moment, his team would come grab me, and we'd have ten minutes, at most, to do a halftime interview in a suite overflowing with people.

Stephen Miller, a regular guest on the radio program, and a surefire top aide should Trump win the election, came outside to chat with me. Miller, a bald savant of border law with an underrated sense of humor and a deep affection for old-school American pop culture (his favorite movie was *Bloodsport*, and he absolutely loved the *Cobra Kai* TV show, which was a modern-day spin-off of the 1980s classic *Karate Kid* movie), wanted me to know Trump was fired up about the NFL kickoff rule change. "Every game, he talks about it all the time. He thinks it's awful. Ask him about it. He'll be excited to talk about it."

Halftime inched closer. Alabama continued to dominate. My son was ecstatic. "We own Georgia," he exulted.

"OK, it's time," said one of the Secret Service agents, coming to grab us and bring us back into the maelstrom of the suite.

It's packed, hot, festive. Trump has barely been able to watch the game because there has been a constant flow of guests since he arrived. He's in a full suit, red tie. Ever the showman, he loves the backdrop, the stadium at night. He wants all the elected officials gathered around him, the senators and Herschel Walker. The lights are bright. We barely have time to test the audio and video and then, boom, we're off.

Interviews with Trump are impossible to manage beyond the first question because, unlike most politicians, he answers far more than you ask, and sometimes his answer might have nothing to do with what you've asked him at all. You might ask him about border policy, for instance, and from there he's off on a wild ride about NFL kickoffs, how much he won the state of Alabama by, what he remembers about Herschel Walker's football career, and why he's always believed sharks are the most terrifying animals in the world.

Oh and it's not just the OutKick cameras recording my interview. Trump is also traveling with Tucker Carlson's documentary team. So while we are interviewing Trump, my interview of Trump is also a big part of *The Art of the Surge*. The minute the interview ends, they're interviewing me about the interview, which is vintage Trump. A story about the interview becomes its own story too.

No one has ever been better at managing the media cycle than him. In fact, no one is even close. The particular genius of Trump, unique among all politicians, is he doesn't concern himself with the reactions to anything he says, because he moves so quickly he overloads the media's ability to contextualize what it is he says that actually matters. He has conquered the news cycle by refusing to ever slow down. He legitimately outworks the media trying to cover him. They don't have the energy to move at Trump speed.

Throughout 2016 Trump's career was constantly pronounced over. There was always something that was going to end his campaign, whether it was saying Megyn Kelly had blood coming out of her eyes—remember that one back in the summer of 2015?—to the aforementioned *Access Hollywood* tape.

But none of them have ever stuck.

Because Trump moves too rapidly for any one thing to stick to him. And it's not just true in the media context; it's also true with the man himself.

As soon as the interview is over, Trump's back to working the room, shaking hands, posing for photos. My fourteen-year-old son is beside him now. "You're a good-looking young man," he says to my son. "Your mom must be good-looking because you're way better looking than this guy." He gestures back to me.

My fourteen-year-old loves it.

This is the thing about Trump that no one really gets. He's phenomenal at personal interaction, uniquely talented at it. The guy rolls into a fast-food restaurant, buys some hamburgers, and wins over everyone in the process. That's not easy to do. Most politicians are bad at it; they don't have the ability to connect. Trump can make you think you matter more to him than anyone in the room.

It's a gift.

Trump poses for a photo with me and tells everyone around what a great interview I'd just done. "Great interview," he says. "Not easy to do interviews like this. You were great. Bit of a DeSantis guy but just a bit. Still great."

I mentioned my wife's experience with Trump earlier in this chapter and how she made the decision to vote for him after meeting him in the 2020 Oval Office. She's met Trump three times in person, but she's also met many other politicians too.

Back in January of 2023, we traveled to Florida for Ron DeSantis's inaugural ball. We were both very impressed with how well DeSantis handled Covid. For my money, DeSantis was the best possible governor during Covid. He got almost everything right. But that night of his inauguration, DeSantis was nowhere to be found in the VIP room at his own celebratory ball.

Because he'd left earlier in the evening.

The DeSantis team, to their credit, was phenomenal. They'd done everything right, reached out to people like me, who had been strong supporters of the governor's reelection, and invited us to the event. (I've met Ron DeSantis many times in person and like him. Like I said, he's been a great governor for Florida. I would vote for him for governor in a heartbeat, maybe president one day too.)

But he left his own party early that night.

Left behind working the crowd were his parents—fantastic people—his college baseball coach, his uncle, his childhood priest, many of the people who were very important in the governor's life. All of them spoke glowingly about him at his own inaugural ball.

But the governor was nowhere to be found.

He hadn't stayed to work the VIP room. And, honestly, it wasn't even that late, well before midnight, probably around 9:30 or 10:00 P.M.

Trump would have still been there.

My wife turned to me. "Trump's going to kill him," she said. "He would be at this party until he'd shaken every hand and posed for every photo."

I told her that she was probably overreacting a bit, maybe DeSantis was just tired, maybe he didn't feel well.

"No," she said, "it's a big deal. He should have been here. Trump's going to kill him."

She was right.

And here was Trump, having vanquished DeSantis and all his other Republican challengers, now the nominee for president for a remarkable third straight presidential election, in his absolute element, at halftime of a college football game. He won't leave, keeps finding another hand to shake. The staffers are all trying to get him out of the suite, to keep him moving, but there's always another hand, another photo. Trump lives for this. He loves it, the crowds, the adulation, the energy in a room the moment he walks in.

For some people, this would all be exhausting, but on this night in Tuscaloosa, you get the sense Trump would have posed with every fan in the stadium if he could have. He didn't want the night to end. Ultimately it's impossible to fake joy, and this is Trump in his element. There is nothing else he would have rather been doing.

He was made for it.

Kid Rock, a rockstar who has pretty good energy, turns to me, pointing at Trump he says, "He's just built different."

"He's going to win," I say to my son, "and he's going to win by more than he's ever won before."

Trump leaves the suite. The energy vanishes.

It's halftime, and the carnival of lights is on the move. Down the stadium corridor, everyone, sorority girls in their best dresses, grandmas clutching their houndstooth purses, grown men in crimson jackets, all of them are moving in the churn of the Trump flood, craning their necks, snapping photos at awkward angles. Everyone is trying to glimpse a moment of history. The election is six weeks away, and the country is at stake.

But, first, a game has to be won.

"Dad," says my Bama fan son, "can we go back to our seats and watch the second half now?"

ON THE FINAL SATURDAY BEFORE THE ELECTION, I traveled to Pennsylvania for the Ohio State-Penn State game in Happy Valley to campaign with Dave McCormick for the Pennsylvania Senate race. McCormick would go on to win his Senate race by around twenty thousand votes. That morning on the drive to the game, McCormick put his chief political strategist on the phone. "No bullshit," said Mark Harris. "I'm looking at the early voting numbers. They aren't getting what they need." I asked him for his prediction of what would happen on Tuesday.

"Trump's going to win by two to three points, and we're going to win by one," he said.

Dave McCormick hopped in. "He doesn't tell us only positive things."

"No," he said, "I'm not an overly optimistic person. I hate being optimistic, in fact. But the numbers aren't there for Kamala or for Casey. They're going to need an election-day turnout like never before to win."

He was close to right, closer to right than anyone I heard make predictions about the most crucial state of all. Trump would go on to win Pennsylvania by 120,000 votes, by 1.7 percent, and McCormick would hold on to win his Senate seat over the incumbent Bob Casey by 15,000 votes, 48.82 percent to 48.60 percent.

But that would be three days in the future.

On that bright, sunny Saturday morning as we drove into Happy Valley to spend the day tailgating before the football game kicked off at noon, I turned to Dave McCormick and said, "Look at all the Trump flags."

They were everywhere at tailgates. Ohio State and Penn State fans may have been on opposite sides of the football game, but they were on the same side of the election.

And, again, what struck me the most was the youth of the Trump supporters. We shook hands and posed with Trump fans of all ages. There were MAGA hats everywhere, but there was virtually no presence on the ground for Kamala at all. Amazingly, not one single person heckled us all day as we tailgated outside Beaver Stadium and then made our way around the stadium suites to greet people too.

That day as I parted with Dave and his wife, Dina, I told them I'd seen enough. "You guys are going to win, and Trump's going to win too," I said. "Enjoy the next several days. You've got this."

I'd been arguing for years leading up to the 2024 race that it would be a Big Ten election. The race was going to come down to Pennsylvania, Michigan, and Wisconsin. If Trump could win just one of the three, I felt like he would win the election.

I texted one of my Democrat friends as I settled onto the plane to fly back to Nashville that afternoon.

"You," I texted him, "are fucked. Trump is winning Pennsylvania."

CHAPTER 8

Fight, Fight, Fight

I BELIEVE THE MOMENT TRUMP WON male voters of all races was on July 13 in Butler, Pennsylvania. I think it was the single moment, maybe in my entire life, when every man in America, regardless of their politics, was impressed by a politician.

Trump won men, and the election, that day in Butler.

I'm convinced of it.

I'll talk about that day and the political impact it created in a moment, but this book isn't a cliffhanger. You know Trump won. But it is, I hope, an early historical record of how Trump won. What was it that made Trump's 2024 win possible and how was it different from 2016 and 2020? The answer, quite clearly, is the youth vote, young men in particular. I told you the feel I had on the ground at college campuses that fall, but let's take a moment here to share what the data tells us.

Men won Trump the 2024 election, young men in particular.

Consider, in 2020, according to *The Wall Street Journal*, citing AP votecast data, Joe Biden won black voters by 83 points. By

2024, Kamala beat Trump by just 67 points among black voters. That's a net move of 16 percent of black voters toward Trump, a seismic shift in a short period of time.

Hispanic voters moved in Trump's direction in a massive way too.

In 2020, Joe Biden won Hispanic voters by 28 points. By 2024, Kamala's margin was just 14, a net gain of 14 points for Trump.

Since 2020, Asian voters, similarly, according to Edison Research, have moved from voting for Biden by 27 points to voting for Kamala by 15 points in 2024, a net gain of 12 points for Trump.

In an election where each side often fights for a point or two on the margins, a double-digit increase in black, Hispanic, and Asian voters for Trump was a political earthquake.

And where did many of these gains come from for Trump? With young men ages 18–29 who voted for him by a whopping 14 points. That's a huge victory for Trump by any measure, but it gets even more staggering when you consider that Biden won men 18–29 by 15 points in 2020. So young men moved 29 points toward Trump in just four years.

Putting this into further context, the two most conservative voting groups in America by age in 2024 were men 65 and older and men 18–29, and both of those groups backed Trump by margins of more than 14.

Trump's big gamble, which paid off in a historic landslide, was that he could motivate young male voters to turn out for him in record numbers. And what Trump's young advisers gleaned by being hyper online themselves was that young men were turning in unison—across racial groups, mind you—against identity politics and woke culture. They believed, as the influencers in the manosphere who they had made wealthy and famous did, that it was OK to be male.

They believed, as my nine-year-old son did walking into Target, in boy power.

But how did Trump translate that masculine desire into support in the manosphere? Well, unlike Kamala, who only did one "nontraditional" interview in the podcast space with Alexandra Cooper of the *Call Her Daddy* show, he actually went on these manosphere shows. He did Joe Rogan's show for three hours. He did an interview with me at the Georgia-Alabama game. He did Theo Von and Andrew Schultz's comedy podcasts. He invited Adin Ross and Jake Paul to Mar-a-Lago and filmed interviews with them. All of that was integral. He went to the audience where they were, but, and this is super key, he also survived an assassination attempt in Butler, Pennsylvania, in the most badass method imaginable.

I'll discuss the Trump assassination analysis and its impact on male voting habits in a moment, but for now I want to also address that this problem with male voters didn't sneak up on Kamala Harris and her team; they knew they were going to be comparatively strong with women voters, but that men voters were a real challenge for them.

So how did they address this weakness?

With their vice presidential pick, Minnesota governor Tim Walz.

Democrats really believed that Tim Walz was going to help them with male voters. They gushed over Walz's background as a football coach, the fact that he'd grown up in a rural community in Nebraska, that he had represented a part of Minnesota that was red, that he was a former teacher, and had a background in the army reserves and had served overseas—albeit in Italy, not a war zone, but still. They did everything they could to convince men that Tim Walz was a masculine man.

But the problem was this: Tim Walz was, as I said earlier, the kind of man a middle-aged lesbian would pick to appeal to men. That is, Democrats have become such the party of women that they lacked the functional ability to connect with normal men. And Walz's own haphazard body language—the spirit fingers, the awkward leg kicks, the exaggerated gesticulations—failed to connect with your average man in red-state America.

Remember how Democrats introduced Tim Walz back at the Democrat National Convention in August of 2024? They didn't call him Governor Walz; they called him Coach Walz. All of their signs referred to Walz as coach. They even brought out the high school football team—Walz had been an assistant coach, never the head coach—but they tried to connect with football fans by branding him the modern-day Coach Eric Taylor from the popular TV show *Friday Night Lights*.

Walz's acceptance speech that night even featured him speaking in coach speech. "It's the fourth quarter. We're down a field goal. But we're on offense, and we've got the ball. We're driving down the field. And, boy, do we have the right team."

The next day MSNBC host Joe Scarborough, perhaps the most dishonest person on left-wing television in America, the same host who argued in March of 2024 that Joe Biden was actually the best version of Biden he'd ever been, attempted to argue, "Democrats seem to be the party of the NFL now." Alexandria Ocasio-Cortez went on with Stephen Colbert and argued, "Republicans think they have some kind of monopoly over masculinity," but Tim Walz, "was showing another way to be an upright man in America."

The usual allies in Democrat media wrote fawning articles about Walz's football background. *Salon* argued, "Tim Walz and the politics of football." NBC News headlined, "This Year's Democratic

Playbook Features a Lot of Football." *Slate* reinforced the contention: "Democrats Are Making a Play for Football Fans. It's a Sign of What They've Left Behind," and *The Washington Post* gushed, "Tim Walz introduces himself as America's football dad."

And this was just a handful of the bevy of attempts to write Tim Walz into the conversation with American men. They dressed Walz in camouflage—even attempting to sell Harris-Walz camo hats, which must have been a real gem for the hipsters in Brooklyn—had him wear boots and blue jeans, extolled his everyman looks, and gave him a shotgun and had him go hunting.

There was just one problem.

Walz didn't seem like a normal guy to most voters. And while keeping Kamala Harris away from the manosphere might have made some sense, if Walz was such a perfect representation of masculinity, why didn't Tim Walz himself do any of these same shows that Trump did? While Trump received most of the plaudits for these interviews, Republicans put J. D. Vance on all the same shows as Trump too.

Walz was almost completely absent from connecting with any of these male voters in the manosphere.

What's more, the attempts to connect Walz with men who liked football came across as completely tone deaf when they were put in place. Witness the disastrous decision to have Walz play AOC in the *Madden* video game just two weeks before the election.

The *Madden* video game matchup was streamed during actual NFL games, already rendering it suspect to most actual fans. What kind of football fan watches video game football when real football is on television? Clips of the video game featuring Walz wearing a camouflage Minnesota Vikings hat were shared on social media in an effort to connect with male voters and included one tweet from

Walz's account that claimed AOC "could run a mean pick six" play. As any football fan knows, a pick six—when the defense intercepts a pass from the offense and returns it for a touchdown—is not a called "play." And no one in the history of football fandom has ever referred to a pick six as a "mean pick six" play. Even assuming, as I'm sure is the case, that Walz himself didn't post the tweet, errors like this are illustrative of a failure to speak the common language of sports as a normal man would.

That is, the (likely) nonsports fan staffer posting this clip was attempting to converse with a group he or she didn't know much about. Democrats speak to men as the Steve Carell character in *The 40-Year-Old Virgin* speaks to other men about how he likes to have sex. It doesn't take much conversation to realize there is no common connection. And Walz's own inauthenticity with male voters, far from stripping away male voters, actually rendered Trump's own authenticity more valuable.

I don't fault Democrats for attempting to reach male voters. I fault Democrats for being such a feminine party that they have no idea how to connect with the male voters they need to reach to win elections.

It reminds me of the early days when I started to date my wife, Lara. She's from Michigan, and all the men in her family—and most of the women—know a ton about cars. Like, everything. Her dad and her brother can wax eloquent about specific cars from 1968 and 1976. My wife isn't bad at it either.

Me?

I know nothing about cars.

When faced with a subject you know nothing about, you can either fake it and hope no one else notices how little you actually know, or you can just confess you're clueless on the issue. It has been my experience that most people respect you when you confess your ignorance instead of pretending to be knowledgeable about something you're clueless about.

That didn't stop Democrats from trying. They sent Walz hunting. They had him play football video games against AOC and talk to high school football teams in Pennsylvania. They even stood him in front of a chalkboard and had him mock up fake game plans to explain why you needed to vote for him and Kamala, but ultimately voters, men especially, saw through all of this.

In retrospect, it's easy to attack the selection of Tim Walz, but presuming Kamala Harris wasn't going to pick a woman—even Democrats seemed to recognize that a ticket of two women would spell doom for their quest to pick up male voters—what options did they actually have? Ironically enough this is where Kamala Harris being a black minority may well have hurt her based on the identity politics calculus of Democrats.

Kamala couldn't pick a woman, because two women on a ticket was too many women according to Democrat polling, but she also, probably, couldn't pick a minority male either, because two minorities might seem off-putting to swing voters too. (There were no minority men on Kamala Harris's short list of contenders.) That meant Kamala was down to white dudes. Yes, I know. It's hysterical that the party that hates white men managed to create a situation where they had to pick a white man as their vice presidential candidate. Sure, Tim Walz ended up being the pick, but who would have been better than him?

Well, to me, Pennsylvania governor Josh Shapiro was a no-brainer. He was a popular governor of the biggest battleground state in the country, Pennsylvania, but, and again, this is crazy, he was Jewish. And a strong collection of the Democrat base—witness all the college protests—had become profoundly anti-Semitic. Kamala faced a revolution from the anti-Israel elements of her party if she picked Shapiro.

That left relatively few options: Illinois governor J. B. Pritzker, California governor Gavin Newsom, Minnesota governor Tim Walz, and Kentucky governor Andy Beshear. Would any of these guys have made a difference and connected with men infinitely better than Walz did? I doubt it. But Walz's awkwardness reinforced Democrat struggles with men.

Indeed, I would argue that Walz, rather than strengthen Democrat bona fides with male voters, actually reinforced just how out of touch Democrats were with them. But you don't have to take it from me. Things got so bad with black men for Kamala Harris that they brought out former president Barack Obama to lecture black men about why they needed to support Kamala Harris. Lack of Kamala enthusiasm, per Obama, "seemed to be more pronounced with the brothers."

Obama continued, "My understanding, based on reports I'm getting from campaigns and communities is that we have not yet seen the same kinds of energy and turnout in all corners of our neighborhoods and communities as we saw when I was running. And you're coming up with all kinds of reasons and excuses. I've got a problem with that.

"Part of it makes me think—and I'm speaking to men directly—part of it makes me think that, well, you just aren't feeling the idea of having a woman as president, and you're coming up with other alternatives and other reasons for that."

Ah, yes, when all else fails, simply have Obama lecture black men to convince them to vote for Kamala. That'll do the trick.

Only, of course, it didn't.

In fact, black men broke for Trump at a higher rate than any Republican presidential candidate since the civil rights era.

Which is why the selection of Tim Walz, in many ways, actually magnified the stakes of the gamble Trump's team was undertaking. The Trump team's play in the manosphere was clear: They believed young men were receptive to the argument Trump was making. That might well be true, but in every political campaign, there's only so much time. Time is, by far, the most valuable asset of all. And generally speaking, young men didn't show up to vote.

What if Trump was right—that young men did believe in his argument—but they simply weren't going to show up and vote like they typically didn't show up and vote? In other words, could Trump be right about his appeal with young men and still not mobilize enough of them?

It was a risky bet to go all in on young men as part of a key media strategy, but I think Trump's advisers had a thesis they believed was true: Trump's response at Butler, Pennsylvania, forever wedded him to young men because of how courageous it was. Let's talk about that day now.

NEVER TAKE DAYS OFF.

Ever.

But on Saturday July 13, knowing I was headed to Milwaukee for the Republican National Convention the next day and with my family out of town, I decided to head over to a friend's pool, have a few beers, and just relax.

After all, it was a lazy Saturday in the summer, the day before everyone was set to travel to Milwaukee for the convention. What could possibly happen?

So I hung out by his pool, had a few beers, and then when it got too hot, we decided to head back up to his place and chill out before grabbing an early dinner in downtown Nashville. As luck would have it, my host, Jonathan Hutton, who does a show for us on the OutKick network, flipped on the television to Fox News at the exact moment, virtually, that the shots rang out in Pennsylvania. We sat in stunned silence as we watched Trump sink behind the podium and then rise up, scream, "Fight, fight, fight!" and be carried off the stage by his Secret Service agents.

My phone immediately blew up as everyone became aware of the assassination attempt. My blood was boiling, and I had Hutton record an immediate reaction video from me. It's one of the most watched videos I've ever posted. There I was in a bathing suit and flip-flops, furious at what had seemed eminently predictable to me, that with Trump leading in the polls, it was inevitable someone would try to kill him. In fact, I'd spent much of the prior week begging for Trump to have his security detail tripled. It just felt so clear to me this attempt was coming.

As I write this eight months after that assassination attempt, I can't help but feel as if our country escaped disaster by a quarter of an inch. Because if Trump doesn't turn at the last possible instant to look at the chart behind him, he's assassinated on live television. The nation wouldn't recover for generations. Even today, the psychic injury from John F. Kennedy's assassination remains. Trump's assassination would have been an even more devastating moment for the country. Would any of us have ever believed that a reclusive young man from rural Pennsylvania was the lone gunman? Or that the Secret Service had unintentionally engaged in grave mismanagement by allowing this assassin to have a clear shot from a rooftop at a president only a short distance away? I'll be honest with you; I wouldn't have believed it.

And I bet you wouldn't have either.

Many of us would have believed for the rest of our lives that Trump was set up to be killed on that day, that a vast conspiracy had made it possible.

That Saturday, America's future hung in the balance. Trump survived, I believe, thanks to divine providence and created one of the most iconic moments for any president in history by reacting in the most badass manner possible to an assassination attempt, a reaction that I believe forever cemented male support for his candidacy and effectively ended the election.

If Hollywood had scripted this reaction, most of us would have considered it too over-the-top. Having just come within a quarter of an inch of death, Trump reacted in the bravest and most steadfast manner possible. Heck, if Trump had remained hiding behind the podium, could anyone have blamed him? Pumping his fist and chanting, "Fight, fight, fight!" wasn't just brave, it could even be characterized as reckless. But sometimes reckless bravery is called for, demanded even. It's often fearlessness that turns the tides of history.

As a student of history, I know how difficult it is to predict what people will think hundreds of years from now about any moment that we live through in the present day. It's why I've never found the argument about the right and wrong side of history to be particularly powerful. Anyone who studies history at all knows that every single one of us will be found lacking, often in ways we can't predict at all, by future generations.

But here's one thing I feel very confident about predicting: Donald Trump's response to his assassination attempt in Butler, Pennsylvania, will reverberate throughout the annals of history, becoming, I believe, even more iconic when the passions of the present day fade, and that indelible image of Trump, fist raised, blood streaming down his face, will be a powerful evocation of American fortitude as long as this country endures.

Long after anyone reading this book is gone, I believe Donald Trump's response to his assassination attempt in Butler, Pennsylvania, will be talked about as a crowning moment of American presidential bravery.

All of us, every single man in America, wonders how we might respond in a situation like this. Some of you, those who have served in the military or the police and found yourselves under fire, know what you would do, but the vast majority of us don't. And I'm telling you every single man wishes he'd respond like Trump did, that we would all be that brave.

In that instant, every attack on Trump for being a coward vanished. You could still attack Trump for many of his political opinions, but you couldn't accuse him of cowardice. And you couldn't accuse him of being a grifter or not caring or being a celebrity who just liked the attention he got from politics. In that crucible moment of life or death, there was no acting. Trump's innate character and bravery revealed itself.

He stood and screamed, "Fight, fight, fight!" and the election was over.

Within moments of the assassination attempt, Elon tweeted, "I fully endorse President Trump and hope for his rapid recovery." With his endorsement, Elon also included a video of the assassination attempt, which has been viewed over 220 million times. And it wasn't just Elon who reacted this way. Mark Zuckerberg, founder of Facebook, called Trump's reaction "badass," and "inspiring," and Jeff Bezos, Amazon's founder, also immediately called and wished Trump well. Each of these individuals—along with many other tech CEOs—would attend Trump's inauguration in January of 2025. But on that day in Butler, Pennsylvania, Trump won America's men.

While Musk, Zuckerberg, and Bezos are multibillionaires, their reactions weren't unique. They were echoed by many American men across the country. Trump's reaction to the assassination attempt was a catalyst for support, but it was also edifying about his own willingness to put his life on the line to fight for what he believed in. There was a Democrat line of attack on Trump that he was a spoiled rich kid who avoided the Vietnam War with bone spurs. The attack was designed to puncture Trump's image as a courageous and brave fighter.

But his reaction in Butler, Pennsylvania, ended that line of attack. And for many younger male voters, it also cemented their support of Trump. It's hard for any president to have a more profoundly masculine moment than this. I think Trump won the support of young men once and for all in that instant.

But beyond the cementing of young male support—remember there was still the issue of whether these voters would show up at the polls—what it immediately created was Elon Musk's endorsement. Given Elon's purchase of Twitter, which we will discuss in a moment, this created a powerful network effect. Trump's message, at a minimum, would not be artificially curtailed by big tech algorithms like it had been in the 2020 election, and this meant, crucially, Trump's appeal to young men on Twitter and Facebook wouldn't be buried like it had been in 2020.

Remember, Elon Musk himself, an archetype of the tech bro in the manosphere, which we talked about in a previous chapter, had not previously been a Trump supporter. Musk voted for Hillary Clinton in 2016 and Joe Biden in 2020. Only in July of 2024 did

Musk become a Trump supporter. That's important because prior to his purchase of Twitter, Musk had been seen as a left-wing hero. His car company, Tesla, was founded with the idea of fighting climate change as one of its core beliefs. Purchasing a Tesla, certainly until 2024, often marked an individual as a left-winger. Even today you can argue no human, and certainly no capitalist, has done more to combat climate change than Elon.

But in the Covid era, Musk had a political awakening. In particular, he saw the overreach of the governments that shut down his factories for Covid as a direct threat to his stated ambition of making humans a multiplanetary species. Without a full and open flourishing of free speech in this country—and around the world—Musk saw his Mars dream collapsing. Ultimately Tesla and SpaceX were about rendering earth more habitable long-term and expanding our footprint to a new planet. But, and this is key, both companies relied on meritocracy, the idea that the best and brightest in our country, and around the world, should be able to have their full potential unlocked. What, Musk suddenly feared, if America turned its back on meritocracy in favor of diversity, equity, and inclusion? Well, the result could be catastrophic because people of lesser talents could end up in positions of supreme authority. And if that happened across the country, American innovation would be stifled.

And Musk's Mars dream would collapse.

Which is why, I firmly believe, Musk decided to buy Twitter, a decision that became inextricably intertwined with his support for Trump in the wake of the assassination attempt. While Musk would go on to spend hundreds of millions of dollars to help get Trump elected, his biggest support for Trump, I believe, actually came in 2022, when he officially purchased Twitter and took the company private.

Earlier I discussed the censorship of Trump in the wake of January 6, but I think it's important to have a brief interlude here to discuss what happened in the 2020 election and how, to win, Trump's 2024 campaign had to overcome entrenched legacy media opposition.

I believe the big tech companies and big media companies put their fingers on the scales in favor of Joe Biden in 2020, and I believe that decision made Biden president.

There have been entire books written on the 2020 election, but what I would like to focus on here is something more specific: how Twitter in particular set the table for the big tech and big media collusion by stifling the distribution of the *New York Post*'s bombshell Hunter Biden laptop story in October 2020. Winning men was important, but in order to win men, you needed an open marketplace of ideas. Which is why Elon Musk was the most important man Trump won over after the assassination attempt in Butler.

As a refresher on this story, the FBI knew the Hunter Biden laptop was 100 percent real. How do we know this? Because the FBI had taken possession of the Hunter Biden laptop in December of 2019. This is important, and most people still don't know this detail. This means that long before Joe Biden was even the official nominee of the Democrat Party, the FBI knew the laptop was real and that Hunter had committed dozens of felonies and left evidence of them all on the laptop. Many of these crimes, the drug use and hooker payments in particular, had nothing directly to do with his father or the political process at all. But as the *New York Post* reported, there were a bevy of details on the laptop that directly connected Joe Biden to Hunter's overseas business dealings, despite Biden's denials. This clearly showed Hunter was receiving payments from foreign companies because Hunter was Joe's son.

A pause here for a moment to share a theory. I actually believe all the Hunter Biden—and Biden family—payments were actually a result of Joe's bitterness over being cast aside as Barack Obama's successor in favor of Hillary Clinton back in the 2016 election cycle. At that moment I believe Biden told his son and his family members to turn on the money spigot. Why? Because he believed his career as a politician was over. And if his career as a politician was going to be over, at least he was going to make some money in the meantime. I think this framing is important. Joe Biden never expected for Hillary to lose. He thought she would be the nominee in 2016, win, and be the nominee again in 2020. And I don't believe Biden—or his political advisers—ever saw a pathway for him to return to presidential power. Or, for that matter, to stage a competitive race for the presidential nomination.

So the money spigot got turned on because Biden believed his political career was over, and his goal shifted from becoming president one day to getting rich.

The fact that Hunter, a legitimate crack addict, could manage to bank tens of millions of dollars shows just how corrupt Washington crony politics really is: Does anyone think for a minute that Hunter was providing anything of value other than his last name and the connections to the corridors of power that opened as a result? Of course not. Now, again, to be fair, trading on a famous name is basically the foundation of Washington political power for both parties, but Hunter's actions were so grossly inappropriate that no one really expected Joe Biden to ever be a political player again.

Even the evidence on the laptop about Joe Biden himself—10 percent for the big guy, the meetings with Hunter's shady business associates—suggests a former politician behaving recklessly in an effort to make as much money as he possibly could because he believed his political career was over.

Then, boom, Hillary Clinton loses to Trump, and there's going to be an open primary in 2020. Maybe, after all, there really is a pathway back to power for Joe Biden. The recklessness of his son's and family's behavior is cast aside as Biden contemplates entering the race. Remember, Biden didn't enter the race until April 25, 2019, a very late entry considering the Iowa caucuses were in just over six months. One month before the Iowa caucuses, the FBI seizes Hunter's laptop. Then Biden is trounced in Iowa—he comes in fourth behind Mayor Pete, Bernie Sanders, and Elizabeth Warren—and in New Hampshire, Biden comes in fifth—behind Bernie, Mayor Pete, Amy Klobuchar, and Elizabeth Warren. Biden gets just 8.4 percent of the Democrat vote in these two states. Next up is Nevada, where Biden comes in a very distant second to Bernie Sanders.

By now it's late February, just before Covid would shut down everything in the country, and Biden's campaign is running on fumes. The FBI agents in possession of Hunter's laptop probably thought Joe Biden was an afterthought and were either planning on burying the story because Biden didn't matter or using Hunter Biden as an example because the Biden family had no power to fight back.

But then South Carolina congressman James Clyburn endorses Biden, and overnight the black voters of the South get in line behind Biden, and it's suddenly over. Biden sweeps to ten state victories on March 3, 2020, and then, boom, Covid hits, and all campaigns grind to a halt. Biden heads to his basement, the presumptive Democrat nominee, and essentially stays there for much of the next eight months, barely leaving to campaign around the country.

All of this background on the 2020 campaign is very important.

Because with Biden in place as the nominee, the code red is ordered somewhere inside the FBI. By the summer there's an Aspen Institute hypothetical for elite members of the media: What happens if just before the election a laptop containing alleged inappropriate materials involving a candidate's family member emerges? And what if that laptop instead of being real is a product of Russian disinformation? The FBI also conducts briefings with Twitter and Facebook employees to warn them a potentially fake laptop story may be coming.

Remember, the FBI knew the laptop was 100 percent real. They had had the actual laptop in their possession since December of 2019. Now, with Biden in as the nominee, the cover-up was underway. We also know that the FBI was aware of Rudy Guiliani having been given a copy of the laptop's hard drive by the laptop repairman, John Paul Mac Isaac, in Delaware. (Remember if Hunter Biden hadn't taken his laptop to a Trump-supporting laptop repairman in Delaware—how many of these guys even exist in that state?!—and if Hunter Biden hadn't abandoned the laptop and if the laptop repairman hadn't made a copy of these laptop files when he gave the laptop to the FBI because he suspected they would try to cover it up, none of this would have ever come out at all.)

Also remember that the laptop repairman, Mac Isaac, wrote in his book that the FBI warned him that he better keep quiet about what he'd seen on the laptop and told him that he'd better not contact anyone. But despite these warnings, the laptop repairman got the info to Rudy Guiliani, who then got this information to the *New York Post*.

Then when the *New York Post* published their story in October, just three weeks before the 2020 election, Twitter, Facebook, and all the other major social media platforms restricted the distribution of the story, even going so far as to lock down the *Post*'s own Twitter account. Why did they do this? Because on a call with the FBI that very day *the FBI declined to tell Twitter and Facebook the laptop was real*.

Again, the FBI had known the laptop was real for months. Asked directly by Twitter employees whether the laptop was real, the FBI declined to answer. (This is why I haven't piled on the Twitter employees as much as others have. Think about yourself in this situation. If the FBI had briefed you in the summer of 2020 that a fake story just like this might be coming and then the story came a couple of months later and you directly asked the FBI if the story was real and they declined to answer, what would you have done? I think most people would have trusted the FBI, especially at that point in time, before we knew all their lies.)

The FBI should have put out an immediate statement saying they had been in possession of the laptop since December and had determined it was real. (The FBI would later introduce the actual laptop as evidence in Hunter Biden's gun-charges trial in Delaware. The Hunter Biden legal defense team, significantly, also didn't contest that it was real when it was introduced as evidence.)

But instead the FBI's silence about the laptop's authenticity in the fall of 2020 allowed the Biden team, and their allies in the media, to dismiss the story and argue the laptop was Russian disinformation. (This, of course, built on the 2016 Russian collusion lie, which was based on a tiny advertising dollar spend—only a couple of hundred thousand dollars—from Russia on Facebook ads. As someone who has bought Facebook ads for his media companies, let me tell you, this is a pinprick of the *billions* of dollars spent in the 2016 presidential election and had virtually no impact on actual voters. But, and this is key, seeding the idea that Trump was Putin's puppet and a Manchurian candidate made the 2020 Russian laptop disinformation story have greater legitimacy as an argument, as the FBI knew it would.)

As a result of the FBI's refusal to admit the laptop was real, many in the media bought this argument it was Russian disinformation because the FBI had been seeding the idea since the summer that a story like this might emerge. Even going so far as to *have briefed top employees at Twitter and Facebook that a story like this might be coming as an October surprise just before the election.*

I want to pause here again because all of this means that someone in the FBI knew the laptop was real and specifically put in place a campaign to delegitimize it in an effort to help Joe Biden win the election. And no one, as I write this in spring of 2025, has ever been held remotely accountable for this act. The FBI intentionally rigged the 2020 election for Joe Biden, and they got away with it. In fact, we have no idea which employees were even involved in doing so. Heck, they may still be at the FBI to this day.

On October 19, 2020, the conspiracy to protect Biden grew, as fifty-one intelligence agents said the laptop had "all the hallmarks of Russian disinformation." That then gave cover to the media to argue that it was actually Russian disinformation—they ignored the hallmarks language and went right to the conclusion as those fifty-one intelligence agents knew would happen—and that allowed Joe Biden himself to argue the laptop was Russian disinformation in his final debate against Trump.

OK, this is a lot of facts. I get it.

But it's important to lay all of this out because there still has been no accountability over this, and we still have no idea who inside the

FBI made the decision to help Joe Biden win. Sometimes it helps me to process information if the facts are numbered to better allow them to be processed. So follow me along here as I try to simplify all of this:

1. The FBI takes possession of Hunter Biden's laptop in December of 2019 and shortly thereafter determines the laptop is real.

2. Joe Biden becomes the Democrat nominee, effectively on Super Tuesday in March of 2020.

3. That summer the FBI conducts briefings with Twitter and Facebook employees to tell them to be prepared for Russian disinformation campaigns, potentially connected to a fake laptop of Hunter Biden. That same summer they also seed the idea with media that a story like this is coming.

4. John Paul Mac Isaac shares his copy of the laptop contents to Rudy Guiliani because he's become convinced the FBI is covering up the laptop.

5. Guiliani shares the information with the *New York Post* and other media, like *The Wall Street Journal*, in an effort to get them to write a story about the laptop. Remember that the FBI knows this is occurring because they have Guiliani under surveillance.

6. The *New York Post* publishes its 100 percent accurate story.

7. Twitter and Facebook restrict the story, and the FBI declines to tell both social media companies the truth, that the laptop is 100 percent real.

8. The fifty-one intelligence agents write their letter alleging the laptop is Russian disinformation, which the media (mostly) covers as fact.

9. Joe Biden cites the letter as evidence the laptop is fake in his second debate with Trump.

10. Biden wins a narrow election victory, which subsequent polling from places like Rasmussen shows voters now doubt would've actually occurred if the laptop had been honestly covered by the media and the FBI had admitted the laptop was real.

All of this happened in 2020.

This intelligence agency–social media–news media collusion led to the biggest election rig job in our lives. And most Americans still don't know all these details.

OK, you may be asking yourself, why does this matter for 2024, Clay?

Well, the answer is that by 2024, Elon has purchased Twitter, and, significantly, Mark Zuckerberg has become aware he was lied to about the laptop, but also about the Covid censorship—Biden's White House team demanded the censorship of certain Covid stories, Zuckerberg told Congress. That included stories suggesting Covid might have originated from a Chinese lab. (Jeff Bezos, apparently, has also become aware of these lies, which explains, in my opinion, why *The Washington Post* later ended its history of endorsing presidential candidates and also why Bezos has significantly altered the editorial prerogatives of his paper too.)

What was needed at Twitter and Facebook in 2020? Someone with balls. Because someone with balls would have stood up to the FBI on the election and the Biden administration's Covid policies too. But, and this is so key, having balls is contagious. And so is being a pussy. Trump's big brass balls in the way he responded to the assassination attempt, I really believe, woke something up inside of Zuckerberg and Bezos. I think it shook them out of pussy-dom. (Bezos in his fifties getting divorced, getting jacked, moving to Miami, and getting a smoking-hot girlfriend was also a sign that he was changing. Buck thinks it's as simple as Bezos got on testosterone therapy, started throwing around weights, and banging a hot chick, and his entire worldview changed. As for Zuckerberg, he's always been a bit of a follower. He goes wherever the political winds blow. Remember that Zuck founded Facebook, initially, as a way to rate hot girls at Harvard. As he got more involved in Brazilian jujitsu, which forces you to grapple with other strong dudes, suddenly he started to extol the virtues of "masculine energy.")

Ultimately, the reality is many people change and adopt different perspectives on life as they age, but I believe in the case of the big tech CEOs, they came to admire Trump's courage under fire and that Trump's courage became contagious, motivating them to finally call bullshit on the woke politics inside their own companies. (Sidenote: I've never been a soldier in combat, but I'm a history nerd, and if you're a history nerd, you read constantly about how both courage and cowardice are contagious. And it's often leaders who instill both in their men. There are countless stories of generals, George Washington and Robert E. Lee, for instance, putting their own lives on the line to rally their troops through sheer force of will. Just before D-Day, Dwight Eisenhower visited his troops to encourage them. My own great-uncle told stories about meeting General George Patton as our troops swept across France. Patton stopped in front of him and said, "Have you killed any Germans, yet?" When my great-uncle said that he had not, Patton nodded and said, "You'll get your chance.")

Trump's response to the assassination attempt directly motivated Musk to endorse him while sharing the video, a video that has been seen, as I noted above, over 220 million times. I truly believe that if Musk's own political awakening had occurred in 2018, inspiring him to purchase Twitter then instead of in 2022, Musk would have stood up for the *New York Post*, allowed the story to be shared widely, and Trump would have been reelected in 2020.

Remember too, and this is very significant, Republicans haven't ever argued for the big tech companies to put their fingers on the scales in our favor. We just want a fair and even algorithm. Musk's purchase of Twitter, which, for the first time, revealed the algorithms in place inside Twitter, also inspired other big tech CEOs to alter their own perspectives as the 2024 election took place, and it also kept Facebook, Instagram, and TikTok from engaging in direct election interference on social media.

Unlike in 2020, when everything was rigged against Trump, the 2024 election played out with no rigged external influences. It was a fair fight. And I think it was more of a fair fight than ever before because on that day in Butler, Pennsylvania, Trump stood up and screamed "fight" three times.

A personal anecdote here, on the media executive side as opposed to the writer side. In 2020 I saw how the election was rigged against Trump by devaluing any positive stories about him. I testified in front of Congress about that OutKick data in March of 2021. By the 2024 election, I had sold my company, Out-Kick, to Fox, but we covered the 2024 election extensively. One of our podcast hosts, Tyrus, who many of you know as a panelist on Greg Gutfeld's Fox News show, conducted an interview of Trump in October of 2024 in Trump Tower. The interview, which received millions of views, was blocked from being shared by Facebook.

When you tried to share the story on Facebook, this message popped up: "Your content couldn't be shared because this goes against our Community Standards."

But it wasn't just the Tyrus interview; it was also my interview with Trump from the Georgia-Alabama game in late September of 2024.

Our OutKick team was furious at the censorship, but it didn't surprise me at all. Because as I'd testified in 2021, after my first interview with Trump in 2020, our Facebook traffic collapsed by 70 percent.

But this election cycle was different.

After our Trump interviews were prohibited from being shared in October of 2024, unlike in 2020, Mark Zuckerberg took note. I shared the blocked Facebook videos story with Donald Trump, and Trump reached out to Zuckerberg directly about it. Zuckerberg then texted back saying it had been immediately rectified, telling Trump's team to reach out to him directly if they saw any issues restricting the sharing of Trump interviews at all.

So in the space of less than four years, Trump had gone from being banned on Facebook and Instagram to having Zuckerberg personally ensure that Trump's interview videos were able to be shared by OutKick on his sites.

What a difference four years can make.

While I'm thankful that Trump can be a direct advocate to big tech CEOs now to ensure that our content is able to compete fairly, here's what I would like even more: an assurance that what happened in 2020 can never happen again.

And, unfortunately, we still don't have that.

What we do have, however, is proof that Musk, Zuckerberg, and Bezos are, like most of the men in America, susceptible to and influenced by the courage of the president. That his courage is contagious. And that Trump's own courage can directly aid the First Amendment's marketplace of ideas.

And that it wasn't just young men responding to Trump; it was men of all ages.

Men were, quite simply, over the bullshit.

It wasn't just that Trump was brave and courageous; it was that there was a desperate desire for a brave and courageous leader to combat the woke insanity taking over the country. Yes, Musk's endorsement in the wake of the assassination was transformative, but the signs of a growing backlash had been brewing for at least a year, even when it came to the beers men would choose to drink.

CHAPTER 9

Bud Light Implodes

O N APRIL 1, 2023, Bud Light lit its entire brand on fire with a decision that probably seemed relatively inconsequential to the company's marketing leaders at the time. They sent a collection of Bud Light beers to Dylan Mulvaney, a man celebrating one year of pretending to be a woman. Mulvaney's image was featured on the beer cans. In an Instagram video, Mulvaney, dressed for some reason as the Audrey Hepburn character from the movie *Breakfast at Tiffany's*, stated, "So, I kept hearing about this thing called March Madness, and I thought we were all just having a hectic month! But it turns out it has something to do with sports. And I'm not sure exactly which sport, but either way it's a cause to celebrate." Mulvaney then said basketball fans had a chance to win $15,000 in the beer contest.

The backlash was intense with conservative beer drinkers turning on Bud Light almost immediately. The controversy grew when comments from the beer's director of marketing, Alissa Heinerscheid, made a week before the Mulvaney partnership, also went viral: "This brand is in decline. It has been in decline for a really long time. And if we do not attract young drinkers to come and drink this brand, there will be no future for Bud Light. It's like, we need to evolve and elevate this incredibly iconic brand. And my, what I brought to that was a belief in, OK, what does evolve and elevate mean? It means inclusivity. It means shifting the tone. It means having a campaign that's truly inclusive and feels lighter and brighter and different and appeals to women and to men." But that wasn't all. She also condemned the existing Bud Light drinker. "We had this hangover, I mean, Bud Light had been kind of a brand of fratty, kind of out-of-touch humor, and it was really important that we had another approach."

While Bud Light fired Heinerscheid and has attempted to rebrand aggressively—spending massive amounts to sponsor the UFC and the NFL, for instance, including multiple Super Bowl ads—the damage has so far been impossible to repair. Beer drinkers have moved on to other brands, leading to a 30 to 40 percent decline in the beer's consumption. I'll explain why I think this boycott was so significant in a moment but first a story from my own neighborhood. In early May of 2023, just over a month after the boycott began, I attended a concert in my Nashville-area neighborhood.

The concert, which is a yearly event in my neighborhood, brings a thousand or so people to enjoy music in early May. It has a football game vibe, with many people treating it as the equivalent of a college football tailgate in the spring. That year one cooler near where I was tailgating was filled to the brim with beers, three different brands: Yuengling, Michelob Ultra, and Bud Light. Anyone could pick the beer of their choice out of the cooler, and there were relatively even amounts of each beer.

I took a video of the beer cooler at 6:45 P.M. and then came back at 10:15 P.M. to see what was left. The result? Every beer was gone, and only Bud Light, which appeared mostly untouched, was left. Now, was this a scientific experiment that proved anything beyond a shadow of a doubt? Of course not. But it did suggest that many people were making a conscious choice to avoid being seen drinking Bud Light.

This experiment, which went viral on Twitter/X, with over 2.5 million people watching these videos, would later be reflected in other results online, and data would rapidly reflect that not only did Bud Light lose significant market share but competing brands like Miller Lite and Coors Light surged in popularity. That is, consumers were choosing other light beers over Bud Light. Indeed, May of 2023 would become the worst sales month in Bud Light history, dropping a whopping 28 percent, while Coors Light and Miller Lite saw market share gains of 16 percent and 15 percent, respectively. What's more, the impact extended beyond Bud Light, leading to a 16 percent decline in Budweiser, 12 percent in Busch, and 10 percent in Michelob Ultra brands too.

And it wasn't just Budweiser beers either. Bud Light rapidly gave up its overall status as the most popular beer in America, being replaced by Modelo. By the July 4th weekend, Bud Light had fallen from the most popular beer in America to the fourteenth most sold beer, a plummet the likes of which no beer brand had ever come close to seeing. As of this writing, two years after the ill-fated decision to send Dylan Mulvaney the Bud Light–branded cans, Bud Light's brand is still in the tank, down 30 percent in sales compared to before the Mulvaney partnership.

Earlier I talked about the NBA's ratings collapse based on their embrace of woke sports, but the Bud Light boycott is now the most successful consumer boycott of any brand in history. Essentially, the brand is dead, all as a result of one marketing decision. So what happened here and what lessons did it provide both for the Trump campaign and also for woke branding in general? And also, why was this boycott so much more successful than any other consumer boycott in history? I'll take the second question first and then I'll explain why I believe the Trump campaign learned quite a lot from this story too.

So why did the boycott work so well? I have four primary reasons.

1. Bud Light doesn't taste that much different from Coors Light or Miller Lite.

Every time I write or say this, I get deluged with emails from beer drinkers who claim I'm wrong, but the truth is I'm right. The success of the boycott proves that I'm right. Most people can't tell that much of a taste difference between light beers. If, for instance, Guinness had partnered with a trans influencer and done the same thing with their cans, I doubt the overall volume of Guinness would have been impacted. People who like Guinness aren't easily able to replace that beer. And everyone, even people who don't know much about beer, can tell the difference in taste between a Bud Light and a Guinness. But the simple truth is this: The vast majority of beer drinkers can't tell Bud Light apart from any other popular light beer, especially if they are drinking several, which most beer drinkers are.

A brand boycott won't work if a product is hard to replace. For instance, Chick-fil-A is targeted for boycotts all the time. But they never work. Why? Because Chick-fil-A's chicken sandwich is virtually impossible to replicate elsewhere. Even when Chick-fil-A was accused of being anti-LGBTQIA+, lots of gay people kept eating there.

The Bud Light product is incredibly fungible. It turned out no one loved Bud Light enough to miss it that badly when they switched to another light beer.

2. Men overwhelmingly make beer purchases.

Men overwhelmingly reject the idea of celebrating trans identity. Men want to be bigger, stronger, and faster than they are. Almost every woman who says she is now a man is smaller, weaker, and slower than the average man. As a result most men just feel kind of sorry for the women who identify as men. We don't ostracize or reject them; we just don't feel the need to celebrate them in any way. That's why there are zero women who identify as men who have ever become famous or wealthy for doing so.

In fact, the most famous woman-to-man celebrity transition in the modern era is probably Ellen Page becoming Eliot Page. And Eliot Page is much less successful as an actor than Ellen was. A man's choice of a beer—or a liquor for that matter—is a form of branding choice. The easiest possible way to show contempt for the idea of trans influencers in general is simply to pick a new beer.

But, also, drinking a beer isn't intended to convey a political choice, at least not for most men. Most guys just want to drink a beer and watch a ball game. Once Bud Light interjected politics into its branding, many men rejected the beer to avoid being seen as taking a political stance in any way. Drinking a Miller Lite or a Coors Light didn't necessarily make a political statement. It simply avoided the conflict entirely.

That is, Bud Light was harmed both by men who wanted to make a definite statement by rejecting the beer and by men who didn't want to make any political statement at all, men who simply wanted to avoid the conflict altogether.

Which brings me to point three.

3. Partnering with a trans influencer was antibrand and offered no growth opportunity for Bud Light.

There wasn't a single beer drinker alive who was refusing to drink Bud Light because the company wasn't protrans enough. That is, the addressable market of people who didn't drink Bud Light because they found its branding to feature too much juvenile or fratty humor was nonexistent. Legit, there were no consumers to gain by doing this advertisement.

I'm not sure there is a woker industry right now than advertising. The industry is filled with out-of-touch New York and Los Angeles ad "gurus" who are paid tens of billions of dollars to advertise brands they would never consume in their own lives. Bud Light was never going to be popular in Brookyln hipster bars. But it was very popular at college and NFL tailgates.

After this ad campaign, however, now no one wants to drink Bud Light at college and NFL tailgates and no one is still drinking it at hipster bars. That is, the entire campaign was predicated on a consumer who didn't exist.

Which makes it the very definition of being antibranding. It's as if Bud Light were trying to destroy itself.

Which is an important lesson for anyone reading this book right now: Never abandon the people who made your brand popular. You can and should work to expand your brand's audience— that's how every business grows—but you should never do so at the expense of your core consumer. This is the most foundational element of marketing. Taking a risk is sometimes important, but the risk should always be accompanied by the potential for a payoff, otherwise why are you taking the risk in the first place?

The best possible outcome of this brand partnership was that no one would really notice it happened. The trans community is tiny. The audience of trans beer drinkers who weren't drinking Bud Light because they perceived it as not supportive enough of the trans community and would after this ad ran was probably zero. At the absolute best, the audience was so small that it would forever be impossible to note its impact.

Yet Bud Light did it anyway.

And in so doing they destroyed a brand they had spent decades building.

4. People were fed up with woke branding.

Whatever your political leanings, there was a backlash brewing against brands going woke. Bud Light ended up getting destroyed, but if it hadn't been Bud Light, it would have been another consumer product focused on male consumers.

No one cares what your kitty litter company thinks about the Black Lives Matter movement.

The entire concept of brands taking stands was, by and large, lunacy. I say by and large because there are some brands that have wedded themselves to politics since their inception. Ben and Jerry's ice cream, for instance, has been a far left-wing brand for a long time. Patagonia does the same thing. But there's a difference between defining your brand based on politics from its inception and having an apolitical brand that decides to become political.

The former might work; the latter never does.

Even people who never drank beer delighted in Bud Light's collapsing brand because they wanted to send the message to other companies that they could be next. Bud Light, in this world, became the equivalent of the person who gets shivved in the prison yard. It's not just about destroying Bud Light; it's about sending the message that you might be next.

In the wake of Bud Light's collapse, almost overnight, woke advertising from otherwise apolitical brands vanished.

So what did the Trump team learn here? First, that even the power of their own personal brand couldn't save Bud Light. In the early days of the protest, Donald Trump Jr. spoke out in favor of Bud Light and the Budweiser brand. So did President Trump. And no one listened to either of them. Even the Trump brand wasn't enough to stop the viral plunge in beer sales.

Second, and most significant, there was a strong antiwoke voter in the country. Prior to Bud Light's collapse, Florida Governor Ron DeSantis had been the foremost combatant with woke companies, Disney in particular You may recall that Trump took the side of Disney in this dispute; so did Nikki Haley. But after Bud Light's collapse, Trump began to pepper his speeches with a line that provoked thunderous applause: "Everything woke turns to shit."

I don't think the highly effective "they/them ad" in the closing of the 2024 campaign, which we will discuss in a little while, or the aggressive stance Trump embraced in favor of women's athletics being played only by women would have emerged if the Bud Light collapse hadn't occurred first. At some point inclusion becomes exclusion. The lesson the Trump team learned from Bud Light was that the embrace of trans culture had reached its saturation point.

I also think many business executives saw the Bud Light collapse as an opportunity to address their own cultures. It's one thing for a competitor to destroy your business in capitalism. After all, that's the goal. McDonald's wants to put Wendy's and Burger King out of business. Coke wants to end Pepsi. FanDuel would love Draft-Kings to go belly up, but the real threat in the twenty-first century wasn't from a rival brand putting your own brand out of business. It was from your own internal culture destroying your brand from the inside.

Miller Lite and Coors Light could have never designed a marketing campaign that eliminated 30 percent of Bud Light's sales volume. That was impossible to do. But Bud Light could destroy itself from the inside much more effectively and efficiently than any competitor ever could have. That's a lesson that many executives took to heart. Prior to Bud Light's brand destruction, you could at least try to argue that no brand had ever been destroyed by going too woke.

No longer.

It's why Bud Light's implosion is now going to be taught in every marketing class and every business school for the next generation.

But the final lesson from Bud Light was actually, I think, the most enduring. The media could no longer pretend conservative boycotts didn't work. This is where I believe Elon's purchase of Twitter had a monstrous impact on the culture. If Bud Light had seen this viral attack growing under Twitter's prior owners, I think they could have snuffed it out at inception, pretended it didn't exist, and bought off the media to ignore the truth right in front of them, much like the NBA did when it came to its own collapsing ratings, and the story would have been buried.

The Bud Light story was primarily told on social media, and major news organizations traced the revelations emerging there.

This was also true of many left-wing stories and protests—BLM, for instance—but the collapse of Bud Light is the first one that I remember major media covering as a countercultural story emanating, to a large degree, from the online ecosystem.

It also ended once and for all, I would argue, cancel culture as a legitimate line of attack. For much of the Trump era, cancel culture had primarily been the weapon of the left, used to police those who weren't sufficiently supportive of the social justice cause. No one in the Trump era had suffered major consequences for being too woke. The punishment almost exclusively ran in the other direction. Conservatives were canceled for not being left wing enough but never the opposite. For the first time, left-wingers had to consider that conservatives might be able to marshal their own powerful attack on left-wing, woke ideals. That had a profoundly chilling effect on the national discourse. Maybe Michael Jordan was right after all. Brands should try to sell to both Republicans and Democrats.

But ultimately the lesson that emerged was a scary one for the left: Their powers of cultural persuasion had reached their logical extension. The problem with progressive politics is there always has to be a new target. It's not enough to change the name of the Washington Redskins and the Cleveland Indians. What about the Atlanta Braves or the Kansas City Chiefs? The problem for left-wingers is eventually this all becomes profoundly exhausting, and eventually people, like Atlanta Braves fans, for instance, just refuse to stop doing the tomahawk chop at important moments in the game. Sooner or later, progressives go too far, and the backlash can be far more intense than anyone imagined.

Bud Light was introduced in 1982, billions of dollars were spent to make it the number one beer in America, and in the space of one trans-influencer campaign, the brand officially died. It left a haunting question echoing for left-wingers: If conservatives could destroy a beer company over a trans advertiser, what would happen if Trump ran a national political campaign focused, to a large degree, on the question of whether men should play women's sports? Wasn't it time to pivot, to change direction and acknowledge that the woke universe had reached its logical conclusion and a backlash had begun?

Well, you might think that, but you'd be wrong. And the scary thing for Democrats is this: What if the gender divide between men and women, which I think is largely predicated on abortion, isn't destined to remain forever? What if, and this is my thesis that is about to blow your mind, the power of abortion politics as a motivating issue for women is set to largely vanish in the years ahead? Well, I'll tell you what would happen. Young women might start voting as conversative as young men just did.

CHAPTER 10

The End of Gender Divides?

Men, as we have established in this book so far, overwhelmingly broke toward Trump in the 2024 election. I've laid out several theories for why that happened, but one question that remains important is this: Why is there a gender gap in American politics, especially since for much of history that hasn't been the case at all?

Well, I think it's almost entirely abortion at this point.

And I have a provocative thesis here: I believe abortion as a major political issue is on the decline in the wake of the overturning of *Roe v. Wade* with the Dobbs decision in the spring of 2022. Yes, Democrats won some prominent 2022 races as a result—they lost the House of Representatives but retained the Senate and prominent governorships—by leaning hard on abortion in the midterms, but the issue wasn't as successful by 2024. I even believe that the Democrat victories in the 2022 midterms were ultimately catastrophic to Democrats because those election wins convinced Joe Biden he should run for reelection and that the country approved of the choices he was making. Once Biden was forced out after his disastrous debate performance on June 27, Kamala Harris tried to run the same 2022 abortion playbook in 2024—she spent a whopping $1.5 billion in her short tenure as the Democrat nominee—yet she was unable to ride the abortion issue to victory.

That's not for failing to try. Kamala's campaign ran ads saying state troopers in the South would be pulling over pregnant women and arresting them for trying to cross state lines for abortions. They suggested Trump would outlaw abortion if he won the election. They regularly suggested abortions would be virtually impossible to have if Trump were elected. Their goal was simple: terrify women about abortion and ride that issue to victory by driving up women's turnout.

But the problem with that argument? It just wasn't true. And the scare tactics on the abortion issue, which were effective in the 2022 midterms, didn't produce the outcome Democrats expected in 2024. That's partly because the scare tactics that worked so well in 2022 didn't materialize two years later because women were aware the handmaid's tale they had been sold didn't actually occur. In fact, the number of abortions actually *increased* in 2023, the first full-year abortion wasn't legal under *Roe v. Wade*, compared to before Roe was overturned. While the 2024 numbers aren't officially in yet, they are likely to show, at a minimum, that the number of abortions remained relatively constant in 2024 too. That's because the Dobbs opinion did what it was intended to do. It permitted every individual state to pass its own abortion law instead of federalizing abortion law based on the fluctuating opinions of nine Supreme Court justices. With the abortion issue now returned to the states, some states, like California, New York, and Illinois, enshrined far more expansive abortion access—permitting nine-month abortions in some cases, a far more permissive posture than in Roe—while other states, like Texas, Florida, and Tennessee, enshrined far less expansive abortion access, limiting abortions to the first several weeks of a pregnancy.

The result?

Far from remaining the incendiary wedge political issue it has been since Roe was decided in 1973, for the most part, battles over abortion rights have *moderated* since the Dobbs decision came down in 2022. The multigenerational battle to overturn *Roe v. Wade* finally ended and, for the most part, not much changed at all. This means that for generations, both sides of the abortion battle, ultimately, fought over a court decision that when overturned failed to change things much at all in the country. For pro-life activists, the number of abortions remained pretty much the same, and for pro-choice activists, the claimed collapse of abortion rights also didn't occur.

Things ended up basically the same as they were before *Roe v. Wade* was overturned.

Now for those activists on both sides who are deeply committed to the abortion battle, it's moved from a federal to a state issue, and each state can now fight it out in fifty different legislatures. And even in red states when there have been referendums to preserve access to abortions on state ballots, they've tended to perform quite well. Which, to me, means most of the citizens of the United States aren't strong proponents of either side's most aggressive positions: Only about 10 percent of the population believes in no exceptions for abortion even in the case of rape, incest, or life of the mother. And on the flip side, only about 10 percent of the population believes in abortion being permitted all the way to the ninth month. That means 80 percent of us, including me, and probably most of you too, are somewhere in the middle on the abortion issue.

But, and this is key, given that Trump gained ground in all fifty states in 2024, the abortion argument clearly didn't work to motivate women voters to turn out in record numbers and vote against him. Now partly that may be attributable to Trump, who has never been a zealous abortion-focused candidate. Asked if he'd ever paid for an abortion in his life back in the 2016 campaign Trump responded, "You know, that's a really interesting question," and never answered. But I think it's also a reflection of the reality on the ground: Abortion is just not the driving force it used to be in presidential politics.

And if I'm right about this, and I think I am, what does that mean for the female vote going forward? Could the gender divide finally begin to fade? And if so, how can the Democrats ever win another election without completely changing their platform? Because, as you'll see below from the data, men always vote Republican, at least for the past sixty years, they have. It turns out that women's allegiance to the Democrat Party is almost completely related to abortion and of a relatively recent vintage.

Because for much of their voting history, in fact, women actually voted more conservative than men.

Really.

Don't believe me? Let's look at the history.

First, let's begin with a stat that blew my mind. The last Democrat presidential candidate to win a majority of the male vote was Lyndon Johnson in 1964. That's pretty staggering, so let me repeat it: Democrats have not won a majority of male voters in sixty years. While this book is focusing on young men rejecting the Democrat Party in massive numbers in 2024, the Democrat issue with male voters has been pronounced for three generations. Men haven't been supporters of Democrats for the voting life of almost anyone reading this book.

But the gender gap for women has actually been less pronounced. In particular women tended to vote more conservative than men in the 1930s, 1940s, 1950s, and 1960s. Why would this have been? The most prominent theory is that women in those eras were more religious than men, hence more conservative overall, and that women were also less educated and more focused on family issues as opposed to their own jobs. That is, women who focused more on raising children and didn't work full-time away from their homes in past decades tended to be more conservative overall than men. This seems accurate to me, especially on the religion front. Women are far more likely, at least for the past several generations of American life, to be religious than men are.

Certainly as someone who was raised attending church in the conservative Southern Baptist denomination, there were far more religious older women in our church than there were men. Now, to be fair, that's partly because women live nearly five years longer than men. (As an aside, can you imagine how much attention would be paid to "sexism" if men lived five years longer than women and got 60 percent of college degrees today? Yet both of these stats are barely talked about at all. And don't even get me started on the ridiculous "equal pay for equal work" argument when Democrats claim women are underpaid compared to men. It's just not true when you adjust for years worked and the jobs that people undertake. Men work more years and take on far more physically difficult and dangerous jobs than women do. That explains the entire pay differential. Put it this way: If women were actually paid 20 percent less than men and did the exact same work and there was no difference in performance, then every small business owner in America would be a complete moron not to employ exclusively women. Just by doing so, you'd increase your profit margins by 20 percent!)

The gender-voting data, not surprisingly, isn't as detailed on gender differences in voting the farther back we go. (And remember, women didn't have the right to vote in America until the 1920s.) So while there was a gender gap in the pre– and post–World War II voting data, it didn't tend to be very pronounced. Indeed, as recently as the 1976 presidential election, between Jimmy Carter and Gerald Ford, polling found very little difference between who men and women supported in presidential elections. So what changed? *Roe v. Wade* became the law of the land in 1973, and abortion politics became a key component of the American presidential elections from that point forward. Specifically, the president's ability to select Supreme Court justices became essentially a war over whether *Roe v. Wade* would remain the law of the land, and Democrats leaped on the issue to motivate women's turnout for their candidates.

The result? By 1980 women had become reliably Democrat voters.

But based on the data of the preceding sixty years, we actually didn't have gender gaps in our elections for most of our voting history. It's only emerged over the past forty years.

Let's look at the gender gaps in presidential elections since 1980.

Women favored Jimmy Carter by 8 more points than men did over Ronald Reagan and Walter Mondale by 6 points more than men did over Reagan. Women favored Dukakis by 7 more points than George H. W. Bush and Clinton by 4 over George H. W. Bush—this is the lowest gender gap in the past forty-four years of presidential elections. Clinton rebounded to beat Bob Dole by 11 points with women, and Al Gore would continue the double-digit difference with a 10-point margin over George W. Bush compared to men, even though he lost the race. George W. Bush cut the gender gap to 7 points in 2004 against John Kerry, but by 2008 and 2012 Obama won women by 8 and 10 points, respectively, and in the Trump era, women voted against him by margins of 11, 12, and 10 points.

Meaning, interestingly, Trump actually did better with women than at any point in his political career in 2024 and performed his worst against the male candidate, not against the female candidate. Could Trump performing better against Hillary Clinton and Kamala Harris than he did against Joe Biden be a sign that some women actually prefer a male president over a female candidate? That's a provocative thesis, but the data during the Trump era suggests the answer might possibly be yes.

Now, mind you, Trump still did pretty poorly with women in both 2016 and 2024, but the gender gap in 2024 declined to the same level as Obama's victory in 2012 over Mitt Romney. And Trump actually did better than Bob Dole did against Bill Clinton in 1996. That is, far from being the ultimate jet fuel driving women's turnout. Trump lessened the gender divide in his final run for office compared to his first and second presidential runs.

Women, it turns out, liked Trump the more they saw him. Now, don't mistake the data; they still didn't like him very much, but they didn't hate him quite as much. (This would also describe what my mother-in-law thinks of me, by the way. I'm not sure I'm quite beloved, but I'm not hated as much as I used to be. And as any married man out there knows, sometimes it's a win to just limit the hate.)

Now it's still very early in a post-Roe America, but if my analysis is correct—that men are moving to vote more conservatively and women aren't motivated by abortion like they have been in the past—we could actually be looking at a seismic generational shift. What if the divergence between how women and men vote, which was larger for eighteen- to thirty-year-olds than any other age group in 2024, is actually bound to lessen? That is, what if men are moving first in their conservative voting habits, but women are also going to follow them in the years ahead?

Well, if that were true, then Democrats would be in an untenable position in terms of winning elections. If young women, motivated by abortion over the past two generations, become convinced that abortion rights aren't actually a huge battleground in presidential races, what else is the Democrat Party offering to them better than the Republican Party?

That's particularly the case because we know that married women vote far more conservative than unmarried women. To a large extent, the Democrat Party has become the party of unmarried women. (It turns out, by the way, that J. D. Vance was correct about unmarried, childless women with cats being the Democrat base. When animal ownership was cross-tabbed with dog and cat owners, it turned out that Trump won all dog owners, male and female, and that married people with dogs and cats also voted Trump. The only dog or cat owners who didn't break for Trump? Single women with cats!)

Clearly, Democrats are not going to give up the abortion issue without a fight, but what if I'm right, and in a post-Roe era it's no longer the case that single women vote Democrat by massive margins? What if their motivation to vote based on abortion isn't there, and they start to look more like single men? My astute wife, Lara, argues that single women in the future are going to become more conservative because they want single men to like them, and it's now, amazingly, cool to be a conservative Trump supporter. That is, the cultural winds have shifted such that Trump voters are now seen as the cool kids, and Kamala voters are seen as boring and uninteresting. If young women want to be liked by young men, could we start to see more young women donning MAGA hats and voting Republican? That doesn't seem crazy to me.

Single women may put up with a lot from single men, but they certainly don't want to be seen as boring and uninteresting. This is why I think you've seen so many conservative women surge in popularity on social media: OutKick's Tomi Lahren and Riley Gaines, Megyn Kelly, Candace Owens, Sage Steele, Isabel Brown, and Brett Cooper, among many others, have all established huge audiences that consume their online content in massive quantities. In fact, building on my provocative abortion thesis here, it may well be the case that the 2028 election is about women's podcasters and online show hosts connecting with their female audiences in politics, much like shows aimed at young men did in 2024.

Furthermore, if abortion isn't the hugely motivating issue for young women voters in the years ahead, what issues do Democrats have huge gender advantages on? Women and men, according to polling, agree on wanting a secure Southern border, safe communities, good schools, growing wages, and affordable food and health care. Both sexes, put simply, want their families to be safe and want more money in their pockets. Does anyone feel like Democrats are delivering on that front right now? Do women?

I don't think so.

This is why I believe the gender divide is teed up to diminish in the years ahead. Women are poised to become more Republican in their voting habits, and men are likely, as I've argued here, to become more conservative too. I keep waiting for a Democrat politician to realize this, much like Bill Clinton did in 1992 and 1996, when he essentially co-opted many Republican positions and used them to appeal to moderate voters. Now Clinton never won as high of a percentage of the overall popular vote as Donald Trump did in 2024, but he was astute enough to run as a Republican-lite in an era when Democrats had lost every modern presidential race since Lyndon Johnson in 1964, except for the Watergate hangover Jimmy Carter win in 1976. Republicans won the elections in 1968, 1972, 1980, 1984, and 1988. Toss in Clinton's two moderate terms, and they were followed by George W. Bush in 2000 and 2004. Even Obama's 2008 campaign was, in many ways, a patriotic ode to American exceptionalism.

My point here? Joe Biden, even as I write this in 2025, looks like an accidental president. He was pushed over the finish line in 2020, not because of any strength of Democrat vision but simply because Covid happened and Democrats were able to terrify voters and engage in social media riggings and ballot harvesting tactics. These things narrowly carried him to the White House. Remember that Biden only won Wisconsin, Georgia, and Arizona by a combined forty thousand votes. Much like Watergate elected Jimmy Carter, Covid feels like it elected Joe Biden. Each Democrat president, both Carter and Biden, proceeded to overread their wins, enact policies that led to generationally high inflation, and both men served only one term. As Trump said, Jimmy Carter died happy because Joe Biden had replaced him as the worst president of his life.

Trump's big win in 2024, accompanied by a sweep in the Senate and the House, increasingly feels like a statement win. Like the one that heralded the transformative Reagan revolution of 1984. Now the best-case scenario for Democrats, and I expect this pivot to occur sometime in 2027, is for them to argue that Trump was a unique political talent. They'll say that explains his success, not their own insanity.

But so far Democrats have responded to losing electoral ground in all fifty states in 2024 by arguing their loss was just a failure of messaging. That's simply not the case. Voters overwhelmingly heard what Kamala stood for, and they rejected it. Remember Trump was outspent massively. If he'd had even dollars to spend, his team believes they would have flipped Virginia and New Jersey too. (Kamala won both states by five points.)

The truly alarming thing for Democrats is this: What if I'm right and abortion is rapidly declining in importance to female voters? What if women are mostly comfortable with the abortion laws in their respective states and understand that it's now a state and not a federal issue? I suppose state election races could become incredibly polarizing on the issue of abortion, but, again, the laws in many blue states are actually far more open to abortion than they were before Dobbs was decided. If you are truly a single-issue voter on abortion—and it matters more to you than anything else—why wouldn't you move to a state like New York, California, or Illinois and ensure you and your family never face a single restraint when it comes to your reproductive decisions? Wouldn't that be the logical decision for voters to make?

But I'm skeptical of this as a true issue or as a decision motivating state movement.

Why?

Because the states that lost the most population in 2023, the first full year after Roe was overturned, were actually the states with the most liberal abortion laws. In 2023 California lost 268,000 residents, New York lost 179,000, and Illinois lost 93,000 residents. Most of those residents moved from states with liberal abortion laws to states like Florida, Texas, and Tennessee with much more restrictive abortion laws. If abortion were truly a supremely motivating political issue, you would have seen many people moving to the blue states with liberal abortion laws. Instead you saw them fleeing.

Why?

Because I would submit most people care far more about quality of life and cost of living than they do abortion laws. California, New York, and Illinois all have state income tax rates that are 12 percent or higher, meanwhile Florida, Texas, and Tennessee have zero state income taxes. Given a choice between lenient abortion laws or low taxes, most voters pick low taxes. (And it's not just families either, young single people, many of them women, are flocking to red states too.)

One sidenote: Reproductive technology factors in here too. It's far, far easier to get the "morning after pill" today than in decades past. And birth control is widely available and quite affordable. This means that the actual number of unintentional pregnancies is likely to decline in the years ahead too. Again, it's not just the law; it's the availability of birth control. It's possible that Republican politicians overreach in this area and come after birth control, but that just seems highly unlikely to me given how popular access to birth control is and how politically risky that choice would be for any Republican official as a result.

Things are even more ominous, however, for Democrats going forward than just the issue of abortion politics. Thanks to the impact of Covid and taxes, the overall population has shifted in a massive way to the red states in the South from the blue states on the coasts. What does that mean for presidential politics going forward? The current Democrat path to victory is going to become nearly impossible after 2030. Kamala could have gotten to 270 electoral votes by winning Pennsylvania, Michigan, and Wisconsin. She lost all three, thankfully, but the margins were relatively narrow for Trump. He won Pennsylvania by 120,000 votes, Michigan by 80,000 votes, and Wisconsin by just 30,000 votes. This means that if Kamala could have wrung out 230,000 more votes in those states, she would have still lost the popular vote but could have narrowly won the White House by a 270–268 electoral vote margin.

But by 2032 that 2024 pathway to 270 won't exist. The states Kamala won will lose at least twelve electoral votes. That means Kamala wouldn't even win the presidency if she won all the states she won and swept Pennsylvania, Michigan, and Wisconsin.

Uh-oh.

Red state power is growing. The only way for Democrats to win in the years ahead will be by appealing to voters in the South and Southwest. And guess what issue isn't working there already? Abortion! The Southern states have the most restrictive abortion laws in the nation, and they are still adding millions of new residents. And those new residents are voting in huge numbers for Republicans. (New York was more of a swing state in 2024 than Texas or Florida was!)

Do you think that's suddenly going to change in the years ahead? I don't.

In fact, I think abortion will continue to lessen as a national political issue in the years ahead. That would mean gender voting patterns are more likely to return to their pre-Roe habits. And what happened back then? As I laid out in the above data, women were actually more conservative than men. In other words, the real legacy of Trump's 2024 win may not end up being the huge move by young men in his direction; it might be that young women are also going to follow those young men, meaning 2024 was a harbinger of a major shift that will exist long after Trump leaves the electoral stage.

OK, this is a provocative take, one that you may not be hearing elsewhere and one that you might think is crazy. What if I'm wrong about this? Well, the map is still moving toward Republicans, so I think the abortion issue is unlikely to play well for Democrats given where they will have to win in the years ahead. What might still keep young women firmly in the Democrat camp? Their frustration with young men and their inability to find life partners they want to marry.

Remember I told you that women now get 60 percent of college undergraduate degrees. This means, quite simply, the math doesn't add up for all of these women to marry male college graduates. So will women, who typically desire a husband that makes more money than them, "settle" for high school graduate men in blue-collar jobs? Will a female college graduate marry a roofer or a plumber, a man who makes a decent wage but doesn't have the white-collar college grad job that they enjoy bragging about on Instagram?

Well, look out, because I'm about to jump on a soapbox here and start preaching. I think young women may well start to reject the girl-power and girlboss era because it often leads them to unsatisfactory results. Most women don't want to be forty-five and single with no children but a high-paying job. Many men are fine with that because, truth bomb, men ultimately feel no age pressure when it comes to having children. The genders are not remotely equal when it comes to reproductive biology. I get why this is incredibly frustrating to many women who desperately want to have children but don't feel like they can find a man worthy of having a child with.

More hard truths: The looming existential crisis that all industrialized nations face, in my always humble opinion, isn't actually climate change; it's the collapse of the human population. Italy, Japan, South Korea, many of the most successful cultures in the world, are losing population at crisis-level rates. China's population is forecast to drop by *half* over the next several generations. Indeed, China's population has likely already peaked and begun an inexorable decline. Ultimately a baby is a vote of optimism for the future. We're on a demographic precipice right now. There are going to be more women over the age of fifty without any children at all than we have seen in the course of human history. How will those women vote in the future? Heck, how will they live?

At some point, I believe many of these women are going to become angry at a culture that told them they could have it all: be girlbosses, conquer the boardroom, and raise a bevy of children too. It's an uncomfortable truth that by the time women finish grad school to become doctors, lawyers, and MBAs, their biological clocks are already ticking rapidly. I get it, ladies, I'm a moron. I never really spent much time on the age aspect of becoming a parent. I knew I didn't want to be an old dad though, and we had our first child when I was just twenty-eight. (Thanks to my wife, Lara, for being on the ball there.) Next year I'll have a son in college. But I've been the youngest dad at an awful lot of school events in our communities because most parents who go to grad school wait until they are well into their thirties now to have kids.

Which is interesting because my own parents didn't have me until they were almost thirty-five years old. And they had my sister when they were thirty-six. Growing up in the Nashville area, my parents were ancient compared to other parents. I always thought they were so much older than everyone else's moms and dads. Now they've become the expected norm, and I'm back on the young side with my own kids.

Given that marital ages keep extending—the average age for men to marry just hit thirty-one years old, and the average age for women to marry is now twenty-nine—child-rearing is becoming more difficult for many couples. Back in the 1950s, the average age for a couple to marry was twenty-three for men and twenty for women. I know many children are now born out of wedlock or to single women choosing to fertilize their eggs, but the math on women having multiple children gets tough when the average woman isn't getting married until almost thirty.

And if the average woman isn't having 2.1 kids, which they aren't in many countries, then we are headed for a rapid population collapse.

I understand that the single, educated women reading this book right now want to throw it at me because you're all screaming that there just aren't enough good men to marry and raise children with. But ultimately the math is the math; not everyone's husband can be over six feet tall with a graduate degree, a six-figure salary, and a full head of hair. Short, bald men with high school degrees need love too!

Truth bomb: Only around 5 percent of the population is six feet or taller, has a full head of hair, makes six figures, and has a college degree. Most men are shorter than six feet, balding or bald, and don't have a college degree. Men get ripped on all the time for having unrealistic expectations, but I actually think men get a bad rap here. Whatever kind of woman you are, there's a man who's into what you've got. Seriously, there are dudes who love pretty faces no matter what a woman weighs. Guys who like tall women, short women, women with big boobs, women with small boobs. Some guys are fixated on *feet* for God's sake.

Men have super varied interests when it comes to what they are attracted to. It often seems to me like women all want the same thing, especially in this Instagram era. And guess what? There aren't enough of the men that all women seem to want. Which is why so many of them are, and I can't believe this is happening, *choosing to buy semen from strangers instead of marrying actual men.*

This doesn't get talked about enough. Women browse catalogs of men's sperm and look at SAT scores, college degrees, height, and eye color. It's like the freaking NFL draft. And then they pay thousands of dollars to have sperm injected in them so they can have designer babies and raise them all by themselves. And these are some of the most highly educated, highly paid, successful women on the planet! They're so unsatisfied with their own real, live dating and fathering options that they're picking total strangers instead of real, live men they know.

Meanwhile, don't think you're getting off the hook here, men. A ton of dudes are making pretty girls on OnlyFans *hundred millionaires to pretend to be their girlfriends online.* I saw what some of these girls are making, and my eyes almost popped out of my head. Fifty million dollars a year to take nude photos and hire a bunch of fake repliers to make all these guys subscribing to their content think they care about them?

A part of me, honestly, wants to write an entire book on Only-Fans because I'm fascinated by the business model in general. It used to be that a relatively tiny number of women could make a living based off being extremely attractive. And often that living wasn't even that great—*Playboy* centerfolds, for instance, didn't get paid very much money. Strippers and escorts had to deal with great risk and often limited compensation.

But the internet has just created an entire online universe for attractive women to get filthy rich. Now some of you are going to say, "Well, this is just the evolution of pornography," but I think that's wrong. Because most men would go their entire lives without ever seeing a *Playboy* centerfold in real life. And almost no men would have any sort of financial relationship with any women they saw in a magazine. I've lived my whole life, for instance, and never met a *Playboy* centerfold or a porn star in the real world. Women who made these kinds of livings weren't in most of our daily lives. Now you've got OnlyFans moms in every major city in America.

And I'm not knocking the hustle of these women, but Instagram is often the gateway to OnlyFans, and, like, 95 percent of Instagram's business model is how many ways can you almost show a nipple without actually showing a nipple. Now, look, I'm an expert at looking for nipples—have been since the *Sports Illustrated* swimsuit issue back in the 1980s—but it seems to me the commodification of the female body has never, in history, been more lucrative.

And I'm going to sound like a dad here—I don't have daughters but maybe one day I'll have granddaughters—but have any women stopped to consider that what's been sold to them as female empowerment is in actuality just the most desirable men getting everything they want without having to put much effort into the pursuit of sex? I mean, think about it, if you'd told rich men in the 1960s or 1970s that one day they'd be able to scroll through women in almost no clothing at all and send them (often barely literate) messages seeking sex and not even have to take them out on dates beforehand and that it would work well for them, would those men have thought the era was empowering them or the women?

What if what's been sold as women's empowerment is actually just everything every young and rich guy ever wanted from life—a constant buffet of available sex from attractive women—with almost no effort or cost to him at all?

Again, for the women out there, is it really women's liberation if men are the biggest beneficiaries? There was a historic reason women used to withhold sex until marriage: It was so men would get married to them. And so men were then committed to help raise the resulting children that ensued from marital sex. As every woman eventually learns, sex is always, and has always been, the best motivator to get a man to do anything.

Just because it's a cliché doesn't make it any less true.

Hell, the only reason any straight man goes to musicals is to have sex after.

And guess what? For pretty much all of human history, that worked pretty well, until the feminist movement of the 1960s began and ultimately ended up, a few generations later, giving men every fantasy they could have ever dreamed of.

Women make men better versions of themselves. (I'd like to think men make women better versions of themselves too, but I'm not so sure about that.) What I do know is this: Without pretty girls, we'd all still be living in caves.

Pretty girls are the reason Western civilization exists.

Boy meets girl, to this day, is still the foundational story of human existence.

But I do sometimes wonder if we've reached a new world where both men and women are more interested in fake relationships online than real relationships with actual humans. And if so, uh-oh.

I tell my own three boys—frequently to exaggerated eye rolls— that I want them all to get married and have as many kids as they can raise and be good husbands and fathers. Because I'm worried about the population collapsing.

I'm truly worried that men and women aren't having enough babies. I really am.

I sometimes lie awake at night worried about this.

But more than that, I'm worried about what a world where men and women aren't able to form healthy relationships is creating. It turns out that our grandmas and grandpas and great-grandmas and great-grandpas weren't crazy. The best possible environment to raise healthy kids in is a nuclear family, two parents, one of whom is the primary breadwinner and another parent who is the primary caregiver.

And you know who also knows this? People who claim to be super left wing. They all talk left and live right. Just about every MSNBC, CNN, *New York Times*, *Washington Post*, ABC, NBC, and CBS employee is raising kids in a two-family environment, and the wealthiest of them are doing so with their kids in private schools while they live behind fences or with armed security keeping their families safe.

A brief story of my own life experience as a parent. When we had our second son, my wife was working full-time as a high school guidance counselor, and I was working full-time as a sportswriter and on-air radio host in Nashville. My wife returned to work at her high school in January of 2011, when our second son was just four months old, and she would leave early in the morning to go to the gym and then go to work. I would get both boys up and take them to day care before coming back to work from home.

I would get our baby up, change his diaper, and feed him his bottle while our three-year-old watched cartoons with me in the living room downstairs.

I vividly remember one snowy and icy-cold Nashville morning when I stepped outside and began to walk down the stairs in our backyard to the vehicle. I was holding our three-year-old's hand to help him down the stairs while I carried our baby in the car carrier, which would snap into his car seat in the back of our vehicle in my other hand. As I took a second step down our wooden stairs, I realized the second step wasn't snow; it was mostly ice. I went flying up in the air, perpendicularly. I probably could have set a record on the pole vault, and the baby's car carrier went flying up in the air too. I slammed down hard on the steps. Our baby, thankfully, was protected by his car carrier and landed safely in the grass below.

But, understandably, he was screaming in terror.

My three-year-old hadn't moved on the stairs. He looked down at me. "Dad," he said, "you really should have used the railing."

I always think about that moment as an illustration of an experience every parent has at some point in his or her parenting life. You're holding each kid's hand, trying to get them to the car so you can get to work. You've just got too many responsibilities and not enough time. And inevitably, either metaphorically or literally, you find yourself lying on your back, staring up at the sky after a nasty fall.

So that day, and every day from January to the end of May, I took the boys to day care each morning and then rushed back home to write before going to do my radio show. My wife would get off work and go pick the boys up on her way home, often arriving, especially in the winter, back home after dark, exhausted, just in time to get the boys to bed and get ready to try it all again the next day.

It was overwhelming for both of us.

And you know what was the craziest part? I remember doing the math on the day care and realizing two things: My wife's entire salary, nearly, went to pay for the day care, and it would have been cheaper for us to have both kids enrolled at the University of Tennessee than in day care in Nashville. (And this was a very middle-class day care, by the way. Nowhere near the most expensive in the city. We couldn't have afforded that.) But I remember thinking a great deal about the economics of our life at that point in time. It feels like everyone talks about how much college costs and almost no one talks about how much day care costs.

And every day that I dropped my kids off at day care, real talk, I felt like a failure because I wasn't making enough money to let my wife decide whether she wanted to work or stay home with the kids.

Thankfully I started OutKick, got a big raise on the radio show, and ultimately that summer my wife was able to quit her job as a guidance counselor and began to stay home with the kids full-time. And I'm not kidding about this, our lives didn't get a little bit better; they got a thousand percent better. She would say the same thing. Our kids, for sure, were better off because they had a mom taking care of them all day long, and our family life was much better too.

My point is this: The older you get, the more you realize your parents and grandparents knew quite a bit about life. Maybe it was worth listening to them more often. If you're unhappy in your life, maybe, possibly, it's just because you're making different decisions than people made in their own lives for hundreds of years.

Personally, I don't like to identify myself as a conservative or a liberal or an independent, because those labels have shifted so much in my life that they often lack any logical coherency at all. But what I would say is this: If something has endured for centuries, it's probably not because it's awful.

Now that doesn't mean that everything that endures for centuries is worth preserving—slavery, for instance, not a great thing—but as a general rule if something lasts for centuries and free people keep choosing to do it, it probably makes decent sense.

And for us, one parent at home and another working full-time was a luxury we could finally achieve. Now, let me be clear here: I'm not attacking anyone's decision to do something different. Maybe you have a phenomenal caregiver for your children, and you're both able to work full-time and your lives are amazing. And I'm not saying the primary caregiver has to be the mom. Maybe Mom makes way more money than Dad, and it makes more sense for him to be home more than her. Families are all different, and what worked for us with our kids may not work for you with your own kids.

Heck, you may be reading this chapter and convinced I'm a chauvinistic moron. But I'm just telling you one parent at home and another parent working full-time, when you have multiple children, sure does make an awful lot of sense, if you can afford to do it. And given what full-time child care for young children costs, you both have to be making a ton of money, like each of you making six figures or more, for the financial side of things to work out.

You probably didn't buy this book expecting a sermon on parenting to emerge from an analysis of the 2024 election, but I do think what connects young men and young women in 2025 is a sense that they've been sold a false bill of goods, that the adults in their lives are oftentimes not being completely honest with them. And that maybe, just possibly, your grandpa and grandma know quite a bit more about the real world than the gender studies professor at Swarthmore.

So I'm optimistic that men and women are going to figure it out. I really am. No pressure, kids. It's just the entire future of our species at stake. Because if this isn't true, here's what I foresee: If young women don't become mothers, I think most of them will end up being OK. Women, in general, typically make better life choices than men. After all, no woman's final two words in human history has ever been, "Watch this."

But men, well, I do worry a ton about young men who don't become fathers and husbands. I appreciate and understand that some men don't want to become fathers, but I'm being honest with you, I would struggle to find purpose in my life if I didn't have a wife and children to work to support. And I think most men are like me.

Most importantly, I think if many men don't have a family, don't get married, and don't raise children, they can't become the best version of themselves. Because I think providing for a family crystallizes, again, not for all but for most men, the purpose of their existence. Deep down, all men are providers and protectors. It's what we are biologically put on earth to do. It's why we exist.

What happens to men—and to the country as a whole—if many of the most desirable women in the country would rather pick sperm from a catalog than marry and have kids with actual men? Well, I think the country as a whole becomes much angrier and more divisive, for both men and women.

Which is exactly what I think we are seeing right now with our gender voting patterns.

And, spoiler alert, I think Covid has a ton to do with it too.

CHAPTER 11

Generation Angry

A FEW MONTHS AGO A TEENAGE GIRL called into our radio show from Utah. She was a freshman in college, and she told us she'd voted for Trump. But what she told me about why has stuck with me. She said the predominant reason she and many of her young friends voted for Trump was because they were angry at the lies they'd been told about Covid.

This past February I traveled to the University of Chicago, where I met a senior. He said his high school shut down in March of 2020, when he was a junior and many of his friends never went back to school in person. They spent the next one-and-a-half years mostly online. He missed junior and senior prom. He missed two sports seasons. He lost some of the most important years of any young person's life, and these kids will never get those years back.

And for what?

A virus that posed virtually zero statistical danger to them.

Kids are smart. They know when they are being lied to, and five years after Covid, many kids all over the country are becoming aware that Democrats, overwhelmingly, shut down their lives. Democrats lied to them about masking and social distancing. Democrats told them they needed to wear a mask when they walked into a restaurant, but that they could take that mask off when they sat down for dinner.

Democrats told them that if they got two shots for Covid, they'd never get the virus and would be protected from infecting anyone else ever again. That was a lie. Democrats shut down their playgrounds and covered them with crime scene tape. Democrats arrested them for sitting on a beach or going for a hike outdoors. Democrats filled in their skate parks with sand, took the rims off their outdoor basketball hoops, told them to sit alone in their homes and stare into a computer screen so they could continue their educations.

All of it was based on a lie.

If you were born between the years 1998 and 2014, you've lived through a new world. You're actually a distinct group between Generation Z, born 1995 to 2009, and Generation Alpha, born 2010 to 2024. Kids born before 2014 experienced Covid as such young kids it's hard to know what the full impact for them will be. They're still processing it five years later. But if you were between six and twenty years old when Covid hit, you had multiple years of your young life stolen. Which is why I think this cohort of ages should be called Generation Angry.

Anger is the predominant emotion of these young people.

And Trump, uniquely, channeled that anger well for them. Even though he's a grandfather to people of their ages, he connects with them on a visceral, emotional level. The young men, definitely, but also, increasingly, as I explained in the last chapter, the young women too.

There's a sense among these kids that they're all being lied to, that they're being propagandized at all times. This generation trusts individuals, not institutions. They trust Trump, but they don't really trust the Republican Party.

What I've found speaking to this age cohort is they don't expect to agree with you on everything—or you to agree with them on everything—but what they are desperately seeking is someone to trust. And they trust Trump. That doesn't mean they agree with Trump; it means they trust Trump to tell them what he really thinks.

What Democrat is trustworthy?

Again, I'm not asking what Democrat they agree with. I'm simply asking what Democrat feels authentic to young people today. I'm not sure there are any. All politicians, to some degree, compete to find out what you want and then argue they can give it to you better than the other politician can. This is essentially the entire purpose of a poll itself too. But polls are reductive. What if most people don't actually know what they want when it comes to actual policy but are just looking for someone they trust?

Apple founder Steve Jobs has a great quote on this. "Some people say, 'Give the customers what they want.' But that's not my approach. Our job is to figure out what they're going to want before they do." Jobs also said, "People don't know what they want until you show it to them. That's why I never rely on marketing research. Our task is to read things that are not yet on the page."

What many have missed about young men's surge of support for Trump is the life that many of those young men lived over the past several years. If you were eligible to vote for the first time in 2024, you were born between 2003 and 2006, meaning you're between eighteen and twenty-one years old today. When you were sixteen or seventeen years old, Covid shut down your schools and ended your sports and prom. Covid was a foundational life experience for you, not unlike Vietnam or 9/11 were to older generations of first-time voters.

The data reflects that young men ages eighteen to twenty-one, those most impacted by Covid in their lives, are Republicans +12. That's a level of Republican support that has never existed among young men in the history of the party. As a general rule, voters get more conservative as they age. What happens when the youngest men today are actually *the most conservative in the country?!*

Do you remember who young men voted the most similar to in 2024? Old men, those over the age of sixty-five! I doubt this has ever happened before in American history, when the youngest and the oldest male voters had almost identical voting patterns. And what do those young and old men have in common? Anger at the direction of the country.

Think about it. What's the overriding emotion of the Trump 2024 campaign? It's anger. Anger at the Democrats who tried to imprison him—look at that glower on that mugshot; it's positively dripping with fury. Anger at the assassin who tried to kill him in Pennsylvania—pumping your fist and screaming out fight three times is the definition of an angry, furious response. Anger at the world that lied to you about Covid and about girls not being different from boys and about having to make sure you used the right pronouns. And anger that the best girls of all could turn out to be men.

Anger, when channeled, is among the most primally beneficial emotions in all of human civilization. Heck, look at Michael Jordan, the guy used perceived slights to focus his mind and drive him to heights of athletic achievement that are otherwise unreachable. Anger is a motivator. Anger, alone, however, is not a strategy. It has to be accompanied by drive.

Anger, unchecked, can also lead us astray. Like all emotions, it's neither inherently good nor inherently bad. It's all about how the anger is channeled that determines its efficacy.

A story about anger in my own life: This past summer I started to receive letters postmarked from Minneapolis to my home address. The writer said he was going to kill me and sent letters on multiple days counting down the days I had left to live. He started off giving me five days and then, without warning, he skipped down to two days left to live. Talk about unfair! We called the police as each of these letters continued to arrive at the house.

I was hopeful they'd be able to trace the sender and prosecute him to the fullest extent of the law. After all, he was violating my own personal space, terrifying my young kids, and forcing us to retain armed security to ensure my family was safe.

The writer was angry at me, angry at Trump, furious at the world, and he wanted to kill me to express that anger.

I shared the first letter on social media, but when multiple additional letters came, I didn't share those publicly. But I did something that authorities advised against: I talked about the death threat on our radio show. The authorities said that acknowledging this person would make him more likely to keep threatening to kill me, but I didn't think so. Based on the letters, it was clear he listened to the radio show every day. I thought if I talked about my family's experience with his death threats, it would actually impact the letter writer and his anger might dissipate.

And it turns out I was right.

I went on the air and shared that my nine-year-old had been particularly scared and unable to sleep after the letters arrived at the house. He was worried, as any fourth grader would likely be, that someone was going to kill his dad and maybe try to harm him in the process too.

When the letters came, I had to sit down with all my boys and explain the threat—we didn't hide it from them—and discuss that we were going to have private security at the house to help make sure we were safe. And when I shared this story on the air, something crazy happened: My would-be killer wrote a new letter to the house saying he didn't want to kill me anymore and he was sorry that he'd threatened to kill me in the first place. He'd just gotten so angry he couldn't control himself.

Talk about an emotional roller coaster!

From death threats to apologies and love in the space of a week. It was like dating Diddy.

My would-be killer said he was an old man and wasn't very healthy. He was just angry about the direction of the country and was furious that I was a Trump supporter and so he lashed out at me and told me he was going to kill me. But now that he'd realized what he'd done to my nine-year-old, he didn't want to kill me anymore.

Now, plainly you should never threaten to kill anyone in any way at all, but the death threat, unfortunate as it was, wasn't as interesting to me as the response. As soon as he saw the consequences of his actions, his anger vanished.

And as the 2024 election neared, I couldn't help thinking that old man's letter to me had, in some way, been cathartic to him. His anger had been sated. And I couldn't help but also think that for many young men their vote for Trump was the sating of their own anger, a direct middle finger at the establishment that took so much of their young life experiences away during Covid.

Now this isn't to exonerate Trump for his response to Covid—he handled Covid poorly from March to May of 2020—but he was still orders of magnitude better than Joe Biden and the Democrats were on Covid. If anything, Trump deferred too much to the individual cities and states during Covid. The result was if you lived in a conservative county in Tennessee, like I did, Covid was pretty much over by May of 2020. But if you lived in Los Angeles, Chicago, or New York City, Covid was an omnipresent obstacle to your life's normality. It made you angry. And Trump channeled that anger far better than Kamala or Joe Biden did.

Which brings us to the ad that channeled that anger better than any other, the ad you couldn't escape if you watched any football game in 2024: "Kamala is for they/them, President Trump is for you."

I think it's the single most brilliant political ad of my lifetime.

If, for some reason, you didn't see this ad, you must have lived under a rock. Or never watched a football game. This ad, or subtle variations of it, aired, according to ad-buying data, thirty thousand times in every swing state. I'm telling you it must have aired every ten minutes during college football and NFL games. The Atlanta Braves games and NASCAR too. Basically, if you were a sports fan, you couldn't miss it.

The they/them ad shifted the race 2.7 points in Trump's direction and was so effective it managed to increase support with suburban white women and black and Hispanic men. An exasperated Bill Clinton, according to *The New York Times*, even demanded that Kamala respond to the ad because he saw how effective it was. Clinton even raised the issue with her campaign directly, but Clinton was told the ads weren't having an impact. (What did Bill Clinton know anyway. He was an old white guy! The worst!)

Kamala's team tried to create a response to the they/them ad, but her campaign's testing of the response ads showed that they actually helped Trump.

And how couldn't they?

Democrats had allowed themselves to be taken hostage, effectively, by a tiny minority of the population, the transgender community. The ads worked because, ultimately, they were true. Democrats were the party that believed men should be able to be crowned women's champions. And, remember, the Trump team knew exactly who their target audience was: sports fans!

I opened this book discussing the Lia Thomas NCAA swimming win in Atlanta, Georgia. This ad was, at long last, the ripple of that Lia Thomas swimming victory beginning to turn into a red tidal wave. Trump, through sports and common sense, was harnessing the anger over the absurdity of men winning women's championships.

He turned the 2024 election into one big question: Should men be able to win women's sports? His answer was no. Democrats answer was yes. And I truly believe that question crystallized the election, captured the anger. I truly believe Lia Thomas winning that 2022 NCAA swimming championship put Trump back in the White House.

And I couldn't help but wonder, *Does any of this happen if Out-Kick doesn't write the stories that helped to turn Lia Thomas's swimming title into a major story?* The first ripple, it turns out, of the mighty red wave, which would send Trump back into the White House, arrived in a direct message to one of our OutKick writers, Joe Kinsey, on December 1, 2021.

A member of the University of Pennsylvania women's swimming team had a story she thought OutKick would cover, at a time when she believed no one else would cover it in all of sports. So she had reached out via direct message on Twitter to Joe Kinsey, who had been covering the issue of men competing in women's sports for OutKick.

At the time the swimmer, who would later have other teammates reach out to us too, requested anonymity because she was concerned speaking out publicly against a male swimmer setting women's records would significantly impact her graduate school applications and potentially make her unemployable.

In order to make sure the source was legitimate and not just trolling him, Joe asked her to send him an email from her Pennsylvania student account. (The swimmer, Paula Scanlan, has since gone public with her story, so we can name her now and don't need to edit her comments, but at the time she asked to be anonymous.) Here is the message she wrote, a message, I believe, that would ultimately help decide the 2024 election:

> My name is Paula Scanlan and I am a senior female swimmer on the University of Pennsylvania team. I just saw your (Out-Kick) article on Lia/Will Thomas and this situation outrages me more than anything.
>
> The situation is actually much worse than it seems on paper and I was wondering if you guys would be interested in a comment or hearing more information on the situation from a person on the team. (That sometimes loses a travel spot to a biological male).
>
> Some examples of the situation is "her" not changing her legal name from Will to Lia and refusing to get bottom surgery. Meaning "she" has male anatomy and is changing in our female locker room and is still self proclaimed to be attracted to females.
>
> I want to make this clear. Before the transition Will Thomas was an amazing male swimmer. He has pool records in our pool and was SECOND in the Ivy League in all of his events. This is not a mediocre boy becoming female, it is a really talented boy

(6'3" and 190 pounds) that is faster than Katie Ledecky in all her events. This is a big deal and we should not be quiet about it.

In that initial OutKick article telling her story, published on our site on December 10, 2021, Kinsey quoted Paula Scanlan anonymously. Included in the article was this chilling conclusion, a quote from her: "When I have kids, I kinda hope they're all boys because if I have any girls that want to play sports in college, good luck. They are all going to be biological men saying that they're women. Right now we have one, but what if we had three on the team? There'd be three less girls competing."

The story landed like a bombshell, rocketing through the college sports community and surging to the top of social traffic across the internet. Thomas, as you now know from the opening to the book, would, in fact, go on to win an NCAA women's swimming title, but the victory would unleash a tidal wave of opposition that Trump would ride to his reelection.

Public opinion, largely based on the outspoken bravery of the University of Kentucky's Riley Gaines, who swam against Thomas at the NCAA championships, and Paula Scanlan, who was teammates with Lia, would surge against men in women's sports. Even *The New York Times*, as I stated earlier, in January of 2025, would publish polling showing that 79 percent of Americans disagreed with men in women's sports, including 94 percent of Republicans and a whopping 67 percent of Democrats too.

On February 5, 2025, just over two weeks after his reelection, Trump signed an executive order ending men identifying as women competing in women's sports. The NCAA, in short order, said it would be following the rule.

On hand for the White House signing ceremony alongside dozens of young girls in athletic uniforms? Paula Scanlan, who had bravely contacted OutKick to help shine a light on this story, and Riley Gaines, who had become a tireless advocate fighting men competing against women in women's sports. Just over three years after OutKick had been the only sports site to cover the story that every sports outlet should have covered, we were vindicated. We'd won, not only in the court of public opinion but also in a landslide Trump election.

I truly believe that if Lia Thomas hadn't won a women's swimming championship in 2022, Trump wouldn't have won a landslide victory in 2024. I believe that moment, better than any other, crystallized his arguments in favor of common sense and against the absurdity of men in women's sports.

On the three-year anniversary of Lia Thomas's win over Riley Gaines and other female swimmers in the NCAA swimming championships, the White House announced it was withholding $175 million in federal funds for the University of Pennsylvania, which continued to allow men to compete in women's athletics.

But on the Senate floor, also in March of 2025, every single Democrat voted against prohibiting men from competing in women's sports.

Meaning even as we have stacked significant victories on this issue, the battle isn't over. If anything, both sides are even more dug in on this issue. Democrats are now wholly committed to the idea that men should be able to compete in women's sports.

And OutKick is *still* the only sports media site in the country to employ anyone who has publicly condemned men in women's sports. I sometimes look around and wonder how in the world is that possible?

How did my decision to start a sports media company in 2011, a decade later, leave us as the only sports site who would tell Paula Scanlan's story at the University of Pennsylvania? And how is it that OutKick is still the only sports site that would cover this story today? Given that 79 percent of the American public agrees with us on this issue, how are there so many sports media companies fighting to serve the opinions of the 21 percent and no one but us serving the 79 percent?

I feel like I invented beer, and no one else will make a competing beer.

There's OutKick standing alone, all by itself, serving the vast majority of sports fans, and then there's a knife fight for the woke 20 percent with every other sports site. But the crazy thing is this: There's not even 20 percent of sports fans who disagree with us. Some of the people in that 20 percent have no idea what the impact of biology is in sports because they've never played sports on any kind of competitive level. I legitimately don't believe there's an honest man who has ever played high school, college, or pro sports who believes men should be able to compete in women's athletics.

For actual sports fans, this isn't an 80–20 issue; it's a 95–5 issue. And OutKick stands alone on the 95–5 issue. How is this even remotely possible? I'll tell you because sports media is even more left wing than the political media. And because unlike the biggest sports organization in the country, ESPN, OutKick has developed a fearless culture, one where being willing to stand alone, just like my five-year-old on the pitcher's mound in Little League baseball, is a hallmark of what we do.

How did ESPN cover the Trump signing order ending men in women's sports?

With a tweet from their ESPN account. The tweet read as follows: "President Donald Trump will sign an executive order Wednesday designed to prevent *people who were biologically assigned male at birth* from participating in women's or girls' sporting events."

Reread this headline and focus on this phrase: "Designed to prevent people who were biologically assigned male at birth." Holy crap. What kind of upside-down world is ESPN living in? This is legit insanity. But it's echoed everywhere inside of sports media.

This tweet came on the heels of how ESPN covered a boxer with XY chromosomes, a biological man, winning a gold medal at the 2024 Summer Olympics: "IOC 'saddened by abuse' of two boxers facing gender questions," said an ESPN headline.

Yes, of course, the two "female" boxers who are actually biologically male according to their own gender tests are the real victims here, not the women getting the crap beaten out of them for having the audacity to compete against these men.

It hadn't always been this way, not at ESPN, not anywhere in sports, and not anywhere in our nation's culture. As I established earlier, ESPN made the time to ensure they were there for the 2022 on-air protest of the "Don't Say Gay" bill in Florida. But by the start of 2025, the culture inside ESPN had so deteriorated that the company couldn't ensure they were there for the national anthem after the New Orleans terror attack of January 1, 2025.

That Bourbon Street terror attack in the early-morning hours right after New Year's took fourteen innocent lives. Fourteen people from all walks of life and all racial backgrounds had decided to spend their New Year's Eve celebrating in one of the most boisterous and festive locations in the country and never went home again.

The terror attack forced the Sugar Bowl, featuring a college playoff game between Notre Dame and Georgia, to be moved back by a day. Now, with both teams preparing to play inside the Superdome in New Orleans, a moment of silence for the fourteen terror victims was followed by a passionate rendition of the national anthem. Immediately on the conclusion of the anthem, strident chants of "USA, USA, USA" roared forth, and Notre Dame's team was led on the field by a player carrying the American flag.

Even watching the video as I write about it now gives me chillbumps.

It should have been an iconic, patriotic moment that reverberated for tens of millions of live viewers and hundreds of millions more on social media, a testament to the bravery and courage of so many in New Orleans to come together and make their voices heard as one, USA, USA, USA, a moment to unite us all, a picture of a nation united, embracing and rising above our collective grief, a nation that would not be cowed by terror.

That all happened in real life on January 2.

But no ESPN viewer saw it.

Instead ESPN was in commercial break. They missed all of it, the moment of silence, the national anthem, the USA chants, Notre Dame running on the field carrying a flag. When OutKick criticized them for it, they initially blamed it on "timing issues."

Which was interesting because guess when there weren't timing issues: When the protest over the Florida state law aired live on ESPN during the South Carolina-Howard basketball game, every second of the silence was fit in. ESPN had time for all of that.

Later one of ESPN's top executives said not showing the anthem was a "horrible error" and a "terrible mistake."

Both of those things may be true. But it was also emblematic of something else, a collapse of ESPN's culture. Back in 2014, before the Caitlin Jenner insanity began, ESPN decided to make a sports documentary about the response to a terror attack that all brought us together. It was called simply, *First Pitch*, and many of you reading this book right now will know exactly what I'm talking about without reading the next paragraph.

On October 30, 2001, at Game 3 of the World Series, President George W. Bush walked from the New York Yankees dugout to the pitcher's mound to throw out the first pitch. The nation's wounds from the September 11, 2001, terror attack in New York City were still raw. Bush, striding with purpose and conviction, less than a year removed from a contentious election win in 2000 over Al Gore, was followed by cameras as he marched across the field. Later we would learn that he was wearing a bulletproof vest, but at that point in time, we didn't know.

Yankee Stadium, filled with many New Yorkers who had likely voted against Bush less than a year ago in the incredibly contentious 2000 election, roared with approval as Bush stepped onto the pitcher's mound.

Bush, standing on the rubber, stared down at the catcher, reared back, and threw a perfect strike.

Yankee Stadium came unglued.

At that moment, sports were at their best. Uniting all of us, Democrat, Republican, Independent, your politics didn't matter at all. We were all Americans. And we would do what we had always done, live bravely and freely in the face of our enemy's hate.

Bush's pitch is one of the most iconic sports moments of the twenty-first century, a time when all Americans, regardless of their race or politics, came together to celebrate the common humanity of sports and the healing power of competition. The message on that night was clear: America was undaunted; we would not be defeated by terrorists. Games of sport, small as they might be in the larger geopolitical stakes, were important markers of America's resilience, and playing and attending them sent an important message: We would not let the terrorists win.

How did ESPN go from a company capable of making a documentary about a Republican president throwing out a first pitch in the World Series to not even being able to cover the national anthem a day after a terror attack? It's culture. The culture that you create reveals itself in times of stress, when your fortitude is tested. No one inside ESPN raised their hand on January 2 and said, "Hey, guys, let's make sure we don't miss the national anthem the day after a terror attack. Let's make sure we are there to see how New Orleans responds."

Not one person.

I bet they wouldn't have missed a moment of silence if the victims had been killed because of their gender identity instead of simply being Americans of all different backgrounds celebrating a new year.

You make time for the things you care about the most.

And ESPN didn't care about uniting all Americans any longer. Its culture had been destroyed by the woke virus, which took over their newsroom, which took over their editorial, which no longer cared about bringing us all together.

This is what the woke virus can do, if left unchallenged. It destroys everything it touches, even sports.

But a positive result: After OutKick's coverage of ESPN's failure to cover the national anthem and the resulting outcry from fans across America, Fox, CBS, and NBC all carried the moments of silence for the terror victims and the national anthems in their first games after the New Orleans terror attacks. Even ESPN, chastened by the culture of woke rot they had created, carried not just the anthem and the moment of silence at the next college football playoff game but also, incredibly, an entire prayer before the game.

The college football national title game, improbably, even featured a direct message from Donald Trump, newly inaugurated on that very day as president, during the title game between Ohio State and Notre Dame.

While relatively minor, the ESPN gestures, at least in some way, suggested, perhaps the culture was beginning to turn, especially coming on the heels of athletes, almost all of them male, celebrating Trump's election win on the field. Eight years after Colin Kaepernick took a knee, the sports world was finally beginning to heal. Consider the following athletes from a variety of different sports who, in November of 2024, suddenly began to celebrate Trump.

UFC fighter Jon Jones won his huge match, proceeded to mimic Trump's "YMCA" dance, and then climbed out of the octagon to give his title belt to Trump to hold. Christian Pulisic, America's best soccer player, scored for the US men's soccer team against Jamaica and celebrated with the Trump dance. NFL players for the Detroit Lions, Tennessee Titans, and the Las Vegas Raiders all celebrated big plays on the same weekend of football with Trump dances on the field too.

Just before the election, defensive end Nick Bosa celebrated a San Franciso 49ers Sunday Night Football win by holding up a white Trump hat with gold lettering. While Bosa was fined for the gesture, the NFL smartly waited until after the election to put their fine in place.

What's happening here?

When soccer players and San Francisco pro athletes are endorsing Trump, it's more than a blip on the radar; it's a sign that the culture has shifted after eight long years in the sporting wilderness. It's OK to love America again. Significantly, the players were both black and white too, sending a clear message that Trump's appeal with young men extended to athletes and transcended race.

Championship teams have returned to visiting the White House with the Florida Panthers in the NHL, the Los Angeles Dodgers in Major League Baseball, the Ohio State Buckeyes, and, significantly, the Philadelphia Eagles, who refused a White House visit after their 2018 Super Bowl win, now expressing tremendous gratitude for their invite after their latest Super Bowl victory. Each of these teams visited the White House in April of 2025.

Star player Mookie Betts, who skipped the Boston Red Sox White House visit in 2018, attended with the Dodgers in 2025. Betts even acknowledged that he regretted skipping the White House visit with the Red Sox, which he said made the news cycle about his decision, and he felt that was "selfish" because it distracted from the team's accomplishment. Betts said he'd grown and changed since then, recognizing that the visit wasn't about him; it was about celebrating the accomplishments of the team. "This is not about me. I don't want anything to be about me. This is about the Dodgers. Because these boys were there for me."

This makes Mookie Betts the anti–Megan Rapinoe, but it also makes him a front-facing example of the changes in sports. The Kaepernick woke, anti-America era is over. Sports are healing. Fans and players are coming together, united in a common celebration of the meritocracy of sports.

And, in many ways, it feels like fans are leading the way.

As I discussed earlier, Trump was loudly cheered by fans at the Georgia-Alabama college football game, but on his election, he also received rapturous applause at the Super Bowl between the Eagles and the Chiefs, at the Daytona 500, at many UFC events, and also at the NCAA Wrestling Championships in Philadelphia. I joked recently on Fox News that the only sporting event I think Trump could attend and get booed at was the WNBA All-Star Game, but when even Philadelphia Eagles fans are cheering you—they booed Santa Claus, after all!—it's a sign that the vibe and culture shift is truly complete.

In addition to Trump becoming the first sitting president to ever attend the Super Bowl, the NFL pulled "End Racism" from the end zones for the first time since the 2020 BLM movement. We all know the NFL is all-powerful, but it's truly staggering to see that, at long last, the NFL really has cured racism. In all seriousness, the removal of the statement from the end zone was yet another sign of a return to normalcy in sports.

Of course Taylor Swift was also booed at the Super Bowl, something Trump had a great deal of fun with after she endorsed Kamala Harris, but I also think that was significant in its own way. It's not being driven by top-down celebrity endorsements; it's a groundswell of support from regular people. In other words, young men aren't supporting Trump because of the famous people who support Trump. I think young men are supporting Trump, and the athletes are merely a reflection of that support, not the cause of it.

To a large extent, the celebrity endorsement angle of politics has collapsed, otherwise Kamala Harris, who was supported by the vast majority of celebrities, would have won by a landslide instead of losing by one. In the words of the clownish MSNBC pundit Joy Reid, since fired from her TV show, "She [Kamala] ran a flawless campaign. . . . Even Queen Latifah endorsed her, and Queen Latifah doesn't endorse anyone!"

True, the usual woke sports media suspects are upset about the Trump dance celebrations, demanding the NFL punish players for engaging in them, but the NFL brushed off the criticism and said the Trump dance didn't violate its rules. Their left-wing, oppression-Olympics, identity politics worldview was always incompatible with the overriding ethos of sport, the ultimate meritocracy. The best man or woman wins in sports, not the best man pretending to be a woman. Athletes, coaches, and owners, who overwhelmingly support capitalism and individual excellence, finally spoke out loudly enough to silence the small minority of athletes and coaches—the LeBron Jameses, Gregg Popoviches, and Steve Kerrs among them—who had decided to make left-wing sports their hallmark.

The Michael Jordan era of sports has (mostly) returned with star athletes like Patrick Mahomes and Caitlin Clark, the most popular male and female athletes in America, both declining to make a political endorsement during the 2024 election. This is smart, and healthy, for sports since the vast majority of sports fans aren't political diehards. Jordan got it right decades ago when he explained his aversion to entering politics by saying, "Republicans buy sneakers, too," a line I would later use for my best-selling third book, which was released in the fall of 2018, right in the heart of the woke sports era and which you should all go read if you haven't already because I was right about everything I said in that book.

Of course in many ways the cultural collapse of ESPN, if you aren't a sports fan, has also been reflected in the larger company-wide implosion of Disney, which has lit its brand completely on fire. There's probably an entire book to be written solely on Disney, incorporating many of the stories shared here about ESPN since sports disproportionately connects with male voters, but a quick history lesson of the larger corporate culture disaster there too.

In 1937, Walt Disney mortgaged the entire Disney company's future on *Snow White*. Disney was so convinced of the movie's commercial potential that he even took out a personal mortgage on his own home to complete the film. His faith was justified. *Snow White* brought in an inflation adjusted $2.3 billion and was such an astounding moneymaker that it funded the Disney we know today. Without *Snow White* the Disney animated classics don't exist, the theme parks don't exist, there is no company. It created the entire $100+ billion company we all know today.

But around 2015, as I chronicled in my earlier book, *Republicans Buy Sneakers Too*, just as the cable-and-satellite bundle began to collapse, Disney lost its mind pursuing woke objectives instead of trying to share universal stories that appealed to everyone, parents and children of all ages.

You can see it in the stock price. Back in the spring of 2015, a full decade ago, Disney stock traded at just shy of $120 a share. By the spring of 2025, as I write this today, the stock is at $85, a full 40 percent price decline over the course of a decade. During that same decade, the S&P 500 has roughly doubled. This is an atrocious record, an indefensible one even.

The example I shared above from ESPN, I think, crystallized the cultural decline in a strong way, but we can simply use one movie released in the spring of 2025 as a perfect distillation of the company's lost connection with its audience. In March of 2025, Disney released a live-action remake of the original *Snow White* movie, some eighty-eight years after the original film was released. *Snow White* was to be the latest live-action remake to follow others: *Cinderella*, *The Lion King*, *Alladin*, *The Little Mermaid*, all of them were slowly being recycled. Remakes aren't necessarily the province of a creative company, clearly, but so far all of the remakes had made money.

How could they not?

After all, they had a ready-made audience who loved the original films.

Except Disney wasn't content to just remake *Snow White*. They decided to imbue the new movie with a girlboss *Snow White* and a repudiation of many of the details of the original. The seven dwarves, for instance, were replaced by CGI dwarves after famous dwarf actor Peter Dinklage ridiculed the use of real dwarves for the movie. This led, perhaps unsurprisingly, to other dwarf actors (i.e., those who didn't get to play Tyrion Lannister in *Game of Thrones*) protesting their being replaced by dwarf CGI and losing the ability to star in, perhaps, the biggest dwarf roles ever cast in the twenty-first century.

But all that paled in comparison to the decision to cast Rachel Zeigler, a left-wing Latina actress who ridiculed the original film as outdated, praised Palestine, and derided Donald Trump on her social media accounts, which effectively torpedoed the film before its release.

Notwithstanding these awful decisions, Disney poured roughly $250 million into making the film, another $250 million into promoting and marketing the film, and then saw the film debut in the United States to just $43 million, a catastrophically tiny amount given the expense. In week two the tally collapsed to just $14 million. By week three the box office was in single digits. Given that the studios receive only around half of the movie's gross, this means Disney will lose in excess of $250 million on the *Snow White* remake, moving from a profit of billions of dollars to losing hundreds of millions in the space of eighty-eight years on the same movie, a telltale sign of a company that has indisputably lost its way.

While Barack Obama memorably said, "You didn't build that," when referring to American businesses and who deserves credit for their success, there's been much less discussion about the destruction of businesses. Walt Disney and many other generations of creative leaders built the Disney brand over decades of blood, sweat, and toil. Now the modern-day heirs of his business are destroying the legacy and goodwill. The brand they created is no more. Parents can't even trust Disney to make movies for their kids anymore.

And everywhere I look, I see it. In sports, in business, in popular culture, we have a true epidemic of people standing on third base who think they hit a triple. Slowly, American businesses seem to be recognizing how tenuous their brands truly are. Bud Light, Disney, the NBA, ESPN, the list continues to grow such that there's a full sprint toward Trump, even from companies and leaders who previously rushed away from him as rapidly as they could.

Attending one of the Trump inaugural balls in January, I watched the national title game between Ohio State and Notre Dame from a sports lounge. The lounges were sponsored by FanDuel and Draft-Kings. Both sports-gambling companies had refused to sponsor ads on OutKick after our outspoken coverage of men competing in women's sports. They labeled both me and OutKick as too controversial to work with. (It's amazing how the "controversial" opinion is the one 95 percent of sports fans agree with, isn't it?) On the very stage that night, President Trump walked out and ripped Democrats for supporting men in women's sports. There I was, the head of OutKick, founder and president of the only American sports site willing to call out the woke bullshit, standing on a Fox News stage watching the president rip men in women's sports while everyone in the DraftKings- and FanDuel-sponsored lounges cheered him.

Experiences like these—seeing companies cozy up to Trump after spending years attacking his positions—just impress on me how much artifice and cowardice our modern era is steeped in. And it's why I think we all have to remain vigilant going forward. It's great to stack big wins, especially in presidential elections, but those wins can be fleeting without a series of consecutive victories to defeat the woke virus and the culture it creates once and for all.

But as the applause rained down on that inauguration night and Trump danced to "YMCA" on the stage, it was hard for me not to think back to a swim meet in Atlanta in 2022, to the moment when the woke tidal wave was at its apex in sports, and to reflect that we'd done it. OutKick and everyone who had supported us had been on the right side of history. We'd won.

And winning has its just desserts, like an invitation from the White House to ride on Air Force One and attend a sporting event with President Donald Trump, which arrived in the spring of 2025.

It felt like the perfect capstone to the woke era of sports.

CHAPTER 12

Young Men, Sports Fans, and Trump In Philly

IN LATE MARCH OF 2025, just as I was putting the finishing touches on the first draft of this book, White House press secretary Karoline Leavitt texted and asked if I'd like to accompany President Trump on a weekend trip to the NCAA Wrestling Championships in Philadelphia, Pennsylvania, as part of the White House's initiative for new media.

This is a specific change the Trump White House put in place to continue to focus on nontraditional media outlets, the people they believe helped to put Trump in the White House in 2024. I was assigned one of thirteen media seats on Air Force One, and the plan was to provide a behind-the-scenes window into what the experience of traveling with Trump to a major sporting event was like.

I traveled on Air Force One to Bedminster, New Jersey, on Friday, March 20, the day before the NCAA wrestling tournament in Philadelphia. I spent the day frantically trying to check all the

NCAA tournament scores as this was also the opening weekend of the NCAA tourney. In fact, I ate my Air Force One dinner—a fabulous lobster ravioli dish—in my hotel room while watching Kentucky and Troy play their tourney game.

The next day I was invited to Bedminster, New Jersey, to Trump's golf course there for lunch with friends. Soon after I arrived, President Trump pulled up in a golf cart. It was around eleven in the morning, and Trump, driving his golf cart solo, was parked outside the main Bedminster clubhouse. Wearing golf spikes, slacks, a white golf polo, and a new royal-blue MAGA hat that I hadn't seen before, Trump was placing small yellow flags all over the golf course where he wanted new trees planted.

It was late March, a bright, sunny Saturday, with strong winds whipping around the Bedminster trees, still barren of leaves in the last days of winter. Trump paused near the main clubhouse, standing on new mulch, bent over, and shifted his perspective as he talked with one of the grounds crew beside him. He leaned over and placed a new yellow flag where he wanted a tree planted.

My wife makes fun of me because I love trees. Maybe it's partly because when he retired, my paternal grandfather, Clay Travis, spent much of his time on a West Tennessee farm. Clay Travis, who you can probably figure out I was named after, was born in 1905 in Muhlenberg County, Kentucky. He dropped out of school after eighth grade to work the Kentucky coal mines. Eventually he moved to Goodlettsville, Tennessee, where he lived for much of his life, a full-time employee in the Dupont factory in Old Hickory, Tennessee, a suburb of Nashville.

In 1969, newly retired, he, my dad, and my uncle bought a seven-hundred-acre farm in rural West Tennessee. They called it the Triple T Farm after each of their last names, the two Travis boys and their dad. The farm was in a state of disrepair, and for the next twenty years, the three of them would make regular trips down to the farm to tend the land, grow crops, and return the farm to its past glory.

I was born in 1979, and some of my earliest memories are of staying at the old farmhouse there, built in 1884. Still without running water, we used an old outhouse in the backyard. It's where I said my first words, where I would jump in the old spring branch alongside floating watermelons that were left there to cool in the heat of summer days, where I'd put on my cowboy boots and a coonskin cap and walk with my BB gun in the woods, pretending I was Davy Crockett hunting for bear in the deep, dark trees.

One of the things my grandfather loved to do was plant trees on the property. As a young kid, I recall him planting a row of trees in front of the old farmhouse that ran along the old, abandoned county road that used to run in front of the house.

At five years old, I was taller than the tree, and I remember my grandpa, we called him DC, which stood for "Daddy Clay," telling me that wouldn't be true for long. And something else too—new trees aren't planted for the living; they're planted for future generations. Because most trees take too long to fully grow and be appreciated by the people doing the planting. They're for the future, a future when the planters won't be there to see them.

For the next several years, I would have my picture taken next to the trees. Forty years later, the trees across the old county road from our family's farmhouse now tower above me. That conversation about planting trees I had with my grandfather would have been back in 1984 or 1985, when he was around seventy-eight or seventy-nine years old. He would die in 1990 at the age of eighty-four, but what he said that day has stuck with me to the present. It's why I still love trees to this day, especially rows of trees that have grown into spectacular corridors of greenery, because it makes me think about people long ago working to make the world a bit more beautiful long after they're gone.

I think about that moment as I watch Trump, seventy-eight years old, spending a day on his property picking locations for trees, trees that will flourish on the golf course long after he's gone, long after, probably, everyone reading this paragraph is gone too. It's a perfect encapsulation of how I see this second term in office. Trump is almost entirely working on things—the border, the budget, trade deals—that will help generations he won't be alive to see. Unlike most politicians, he isn't thinking about the next election. He's thinking about people he won't be alive to see grow into adults. He's planting for a future he won't live to see.

On this Saturday in March, Trump leaves the tree location, trailed by an entire golf cart motorcade of Secret Service and staffers. He pulls up at the Bedminster clubhouse shop. Inside Trump poses for photos with a couple of visitors and then comes to the counter and begins to sign hats for the clubhouse. He chats with me as he signs the hats—he knows we're scheduled for an interview on the flight to the wrestling championships—and I compliment him on the new royal-blue MAGA hat. As soon as I compliment him on the hat, Trump tries to take it off and hand it to me.

I refuse. How could I take the actual hat off the president's head? So instead he grabs a red "Trump Was Right About Everything" hat and signs it for me. "You know," he says. "It's true. I really was right about everything."

Just then his phone rings. Trump carries around his own personal cell phone and answers most of the calls himself. He holds up a finger for me. One of the governors, a Democrat one, has called asking for a favor.

He hangs up, and I ask him if any current Democrats impress him.

"Just one," he says, "but he's been gone a while, FDR." (Trump has recently put a Franklin Delano Roosevelt bust in his White House office.) It's also a nod to Trump's current status. He's term-limited out but has been enjoying discussing ways he could stay in office.

"Four terms," he says, smiling as he continues to sign hats for the clubhouse.

Waving bye to the staff, Trump takes leave of the clubhouse, climbs back in his golf cart, and continues his tree-focused trip around Bedminster's Golf Course.

Democrats have spent ten years trying to bankrupt, imprison, and kill him, and yet the American public, by and large, has come to like Trump more and more. He keeps setting new highs in approval, and when that happens, I think you get the best version of Trump. He gives off the energy he receives, only more so because he has more energy than most. If you praise him, he praises you back tenfold; if you attack him, he attacks you back tenfold.

The fact that most Democrats and legacy media still haven't figured this out is wild to me, but I do think most of the American public, especially the young male voters who broke for him in huge numbers have felt it too. They see him as their grandfather, and many men view their grandfathers almost reverently. I know I do.

Frankly, I love the guy, and I think he's trying to do the best job he can in the world's most difficult job. And ever since he responded like he did in Butler, Pennsylvania, to the assassination attempt,

I feel about Trump like I do an athlete who is nearing the end of his career but we know is already a hall of famer—does he have one more title in him or not? And I think Trump does. He's like Tom Brady leaving the Patriots and going to the Tampa Bay Buccaneers, the period in his career where a lot of the hate begins to fade with reasonable people and you just tell yourself to enjoy the ride because there's not going to be anyone else like him and you don't know how much more time you have to appreciate him.

At lunch, the guy in charge of Trump's concrete—Trump described him as "better at concrete than golfing" when we met at Mar-a-Lago—talks about the day after the Butler, Pennsylvania, assassination. He says Trump was out on the golf range, hitting golf balls, big bandage on his ear. The concrete guy says he's getting choked up talking to Trump, and Trump says he's fine and immediately asks how the concrete business is going. The concrete guy says, "You know, Bidenomics," and Trump immediately turns to his assistant and says, "Figure out where we need some concrete and put him on it."

One of Trump's longtime New York drivers is there at Bedminster too, and he's a fan of mine. Born in Chicago, Trump's driver wants to talk about the Bears, the NFL draft, and the 1990s era Chicago Bulls. Oh and Trump. He says he was also at Bedminster the day after the assassination attempt.

"That day I just stood and watched him hitting golf balls, and I was thinking, *He's just built different*."

Later that day, on Air Force One, I interview Trump and ask him about hitting golf balls the day after he was nearly assassinated. He shrugs. "What else was I going to do?" he asks.

President Trump is sitting at a desk in his private quarters on Air Force One. He's wearing a full suit, red tie, presidential seal on the wall behind him, two flat-screen televisions (one behind him, the other directly in front of him) tuned to Fox News on one and a UFC fight on the other. The interview, to be recorded on my phone—hopefully—requires the televisions to be turned down, but Trump isn't sure how to do that so the staffers have to figure it out for him.

He's drinking a Bloody Mary without alcohol out of a whiskey glass, a celery stick extended from the end. His phone, never more than a few feet away from him, is open on *The New York Times* app, and he's scrolling through the stories as I sit down across from him. "They can't get enough of me," he says, scrolling through the top stories, "Trump story, Trump story, Trump story, Trump story." He pauses. "Pope story." (The pope has been unwell and hospitalized.) "Trump story, Trump story, Trump story."

He puts down his phone.

Sighs.

I ask him my first question, the question that motivates this book, and, I believe, spells doom for the Democrat Party in the years ahead: Why have young men supported Trump in such large numbers?

Trump's answer to me hits on economics, the border, and Joe Biden's failures. The pitch that won him the election. He closes the answer by saying, "I think they see it's working."

It's an interesting answer to me because Trump sees the motivation of young male voters as being similar to the motivations of voters of all ages. But I don't think that's it. I don't think young white men, for instance, voted 75–25 for Trump over Kamala solely because of economics and Biden's failings. I think it's much deeper than that. Young men—as I've stated before in the book, but it bears repeating because it's so staggering—or more specifically, young white men under twenty, were more likely to support Trump than white men over the age of seventy-five were. We've truly never seen anything like these numbers.

We continue talking, and President Trump's phone rings. Trump pauses to answer it. A week before, a man on Florida's gulf coast, on the 30a roadway, named Marvin Peavy, won his dispute with Walton County, Florida, over his right to display huge pro-Trump banners on his house. He's been displaying them since 2020, running up tens of thousands of dollars in fines, which he's refused to pay. When he won his dispute, one of Trump's top assistants, Natalie Harp, asked me for his phone number. I gave it to her. Two days later, Trump called Marvin to thank him for his support.

Marvin texted me that it was one of the best days of his life.

Very, very few of these stories go public, but they happen all the time because I personally hear about them quite a lot.

Trump is uniquely skilled at things like this.

Ending his call, the interview continues. Trump is Trump. Our interview makes a ton of news, and we land in Philadelphia, meaning it's time to join the motorcade and head to the NCAA wrestling tournament. The presidential motorcade whisks through Philadelphia with zero traffic. This really is the best possible way to travel. The beast, Trump's large presidential vehicle, pulls into the bowels of the arena. We park just outside and walk a short distance inside.

The NCAA wrestling tournament has made a special seating section on the floor of the arena. There are roughly thirty seats for Trump's party, two rows of fifteen seats. I'm near one aisle on the front row. Trump is on the other end on the front row, closest to the wrestling mat.

The arena is packed, the atmosphere electric. It feels like what it is—a big-time sporting event, energy juiced to the roof. I've been fortunate over the past twenty years to attend every major sporting event in the country: Super Bowls, college football title games, big basketball games, Wrestlemanias, Kentucky Derbys, Indy 500s, NASCAR races, the kind of events that make the hairs on the back of your arms stand at attention, where you can feel the energy radiating in every direction, where at times you have to pinch yourself to make sure it's all real.

It's like that in the moments before the president enters the arena.

I'm there first with White House press secretary Karoline Leavitt and chief of staff Susie Wiles. And then Elon Musk enters to raucous applause. Karoline sits down beside me and says they have timed it with television to announce the president and allow him to walk into the arena along the same path the top college wrestlers are using to enter their matches.

More congressmen and senators arrive. Our section is now full except for President Trump. Karoline taps me.

"In one minute," she says.

They pull down the music, it's relatively quiet in the arena.

And then the announcement, "Ladies and Gentlemen, please welcome the forty-fifth and forty-seventh president . . ." and then the cheers are so loud you can't hear the rest of the announcement. The roar is so loud, in fact, that it can mean only one thing: President Trump is in the arena.

Trump, now wearing a long overcoat over his dark suit and red tie, walks out on a green carpet as a deafening roar descends on the arena floor. He steps to his left, shakes the hand of a young child, and then takes a few steps, raises his fist, turns the fist into a wave, and pumps his fist anew as the cheers rain down on him.

As I watch him acknowledge the arena, I can't help but think it was only eight months ago that an assassin's bullet came within a quarter of an inch of killing him. Back in late September at the Georgia-Alabama game, the fears of another assassin's bullet were so intense that they replaced the outdoor seating area at Bryant-Denny Stadium with bulletproof glass before I could interview him. Yet here he is, walking without any security in close proximity to him at all, waving to the crowd, not a hint of fear in his movement.

Built. Different.

Whatever you think of Trump, it's remarkable how he seems to have no fear of being shot again. There is no post-traumatic stress. He seems to have no care in the world at all, fearless on a level that perhaps no politician has ever been in any of our lives.

Now the crowd finds another gear, the sound increases, begins to chant in a deafening roar, "USA, USA, USA!"

Trump gives me a handshake and hug, passes twelve others in his row, greeting each, and takes his seat. This is the fifth consecutive major sporting event where the president has been loudly cheered: the Georgia-Alabama football game during the campaign, multiple UFC events, the Super Bowl, the Daytona 500, and now the NCAA Wrestling Championships.

As I watch the applause rain down on the president, I can't help but feel like OutKick has won. The attempt to turn sports into another prong of the woke identity politics universe has failed. Sports fans are over the woke bullshit, and Trump's victory is proof of that. From a historical basis, I didn't live through the 1960s and see how that era impacted sports, but I do know that by the time I was a kid in the 1980s and 1990s, sports were an entirely unifying force. I don't remember any divisiveness at all during the first decade of the 2000s or even the beginning of the 2010s. It just exploded, as I discussed earlier in the book, with Colin Kaepernick kneeling in 2016.

But here, tonight, as Trump bathes in the adulation of the American sporting public, heck, as ESPN themselves cover the president arriving at the wrestling match, it's hard not to argue that the Kaepernick era is over. That woke sports are over. That common sense and sanity have, at long last, won.

Not that, mind you, every sports fans will agree on everything, but just that American sports are healing. I wrote in *Republicans Buy Sneakers Too* that the great unifying feature of sports was that when your home team wins, no one thinks about the politics of any other fan. We all just celebrate together. For my entire youth, you wouldn't have even thought twice about rooting for the American team at the Olympics. That changed with the Colin Kaepernicks, LeBrons, and Megan Rapinoes of the world, but their era was the aberration, the departure from normalcy, and now common sense was back.

It doesn't matter where you are—a kid's birthday party, a company party, a wedding, a funeral—eventually sports fans find each other, and before long we're just hanging out, talking about past games, past athletes. We all speak the same language, and our race, our politics, our religion, it all fades away to the experience of being in the arena, of being in the stadium. The communal spirit of competition carries over us and sweeps away our differences.

I'll leave it for future historians to determine how much Trump was a cause of all of this woke sports era. I happen to think he was more symptom than cause. And I happen to believe that social media drove everyone bonkers for a decade or more, but, again, that will reveal itself in the generations to come as history unspools and distance provides clarity. For now we've got wrestling to watch and champions to crown.

The first group of winning wrestlers come to take their place on the platform and be honored for their championships. The entire arena is standing and cheering them, including the president. I can see the wrestlers are all looking at President Trump. As they come off the platform, they're looking in our direction, unsure of what to do. I wave them over.

And one by one, every single wrestler all evening long will come off the stage with their NCAA plaques in hand and shake the president's hand and get their pictures taken with him. Every. Single. One.

All weight classes, all schools, all races, all champions want to meet the president.

The young men, many of whom likely voted for Trump, and the sports fans in the arena, all cheer as one. The two groups, I believe, who saved America and won Trump the election all come together in one cacophonous medley.

Beside me press secretary Karoline Leavitt takes pictures on her own phone. In between the wrestling matches, we talk about how unscripted this all is. We have no idea how every wrestler will behave or if any of them might do something designed to draw attention to them and disrespect the president.

But none do.

Instead many come up with creative wrestling poses, including one with Trump posing alongside a wrestling champion in grappling style.

Karoline Levitt pulls up her phone, posts the picture, writes a message, deletes it, stares at the picture. Eventually she writes, "Coolest. President. Ever."

She shows me the caption.

"Good? Should I just leave it blank?"

"No," I say, "that's perfect. And the comments will be great."

And they were.

Trump is scheduled to leave the NCAA wrestling tournament at nine, roughly two hours after we arrive at the arena.

The beast, his protected vehicle, is parked just off the arena floor, and the wrestlers, all fresh off their matches, are walking around the vehicle, taking pictures, marveling at the vehicle and the fact the president is there at their matches, bringing more attention to the NCAA Wrestling Championships than they've ever received in my lifetime.

But nine passes, and the president won't leave.

Nine thirty.

They always want the president to leave before the sporting event is over because it's safer, easier to depart. It's why he left the Georgia-Alabama game just after halftime back in late September, why he generally isn't there for the entire sporting event.

Ten.

Trump is different this time, more relaxed, feeding off the energy of sports fans like never before. Athletes love him. He loves them. This is always how it was, the symbiosis, Trump watching Tyson, Trump at Wrestlemania, Trump literally in the arena, Trump enjoying every moment, the sports fan who doesn't want to leave, because if he does, what might happen that he will have missed?

Ten fifteen.

And then, magic.

One of the biggest upsets in NCAA wrestling history. And not just that, a former Air Force cadet, now wrestling for Oklahoma State, wins and then drapes himself in the American flag. He salutes his president, and the roof feels like it's going to come off the arena as Trump stands watching, nearly one-and-a-half hours after his scheduled departure.

Now Trump piles into the beast, the motorcade storms through the streets of Philadelphia, back to the airport, up in the air, back to the White House and Washington, DC.

Roughly thirty minutes later, we glide in for the landing at Andrews Air Force Base. I'm hitting refresh on the score app as hard as I can for the latest score on the Tennessee-UCLA NCAA tournament basketball game.

My phone is popping with all the alerts from the Trump interview I did a few hours ago. By Monday the following outlets will have written about the interview: *The New York Times*, *The Washington Post*, *USA Today*, Yahoo Sports, *Reuters*, *Sports Illustrated*, CNN, Fox News, *The Hill*, *Mediaite*, *Daily Mail*, *The Mirror*, the *US Sun*, Axios, Daily Beast, the *New York Post*, and others.

It's nearly midnight in Washington, DC, Saturday becoming Sunday, a March chill in the air. It's eerily quiet, and I'm alone at the visitor's entrance of Andrews Air Force Base, waiting for an Uber to take me to the hotel. I'm watching my Uber driver inch closer and closer to me, shivering as I scroll through the box score of the Tennessee-UCLA basketball game, which has just ended.

Tomorrow morning I'll be up early for a flight back to Nashville—not many people have gone, I'd wager, straight from Air Force One to Southwest Airlines—but for now it's after midnight, and I'm in a reflective mood.

And while I stand there waiting on my Uber, I find myself thinking about when I founded OutKick back in 2011 in a Birmingham, Alabama, hotel room and how the site crashed on that first day. And I think about how many people told me I was crazy when

I said President Trump would be on my OutKick the Coverage morning radio show. And then I find myself thinking again, as I was earlier in the day, about my paternal grandfather, Clay Travis, the man I was named after, who loved planting trees on our family farm in West Tennessee.

He had an eighth-grade education and labored in the Kentucky coal mines before moving to the Nashville area and having my dad. Born in 1905, he died in 1990. In his entire life, my grandfather never took an airplane flight.

Not one.

And his grandson just interviewed the president of the United States on Air Force One.

What a country.

What a time to be alive.

EPILOGUE

IN FEBRUARY OF 2025, I traveled to the University of Chicago to speak on a panel about gender roles in the 2024 election. The panel was called "Trad Wives & Alpha Males: Gender Relations in the Blender." The room was filled with young students, mostly female, and my comments on why Trump won weren't received well by that left-wing audience. I made many of the arguments you've read in this book, and near the end of the panel discussion, I asked the crowd, mostly of college kids, to tell me who the most masculine Democrat in the party was. There was stunned silence. I then continued on the stage.

"Mayor Pete?"

The moderator of the panel, an editor from *The Atlantic*, Hannah Rosin, responded, in perfect woke, identity politics, word-policing fashion, "Is that a gay joke?"

"No," I said, "it's just that he's not particularly masculine. No one's like Mayor Pete. He's a badass. Chuck Schumer, is anybody like Chuck Schumer, holding up an avocado and a beer to talk about the Super Bowl, trying to grill? Is anyone like, boy, that's a dude I want to hang out with?"

"But Trump's like a grandpa," Rosin interjected.

The crowd laughed uproariously. I paused for a few seconds to allow their laughter to fade and then said, "Trump took a bullet in his ear and immediately stood up and said, 'Fight, Fight, Fight.' Every man in America and most of the women out here were impressed by that, even if the women won't admit it." (I pointed to a woman in the crowd. "She's shaking her head right now. She's lying." More gasps.) Then I continued, "Democrats, for men, are pussies, and Republicans are not. There are no masculine men in the Democrat Party right now."

As the college kids filed out of the room, they looked at me like I'd just ripped the head off a kitten on stage.

Once again, I'd created a mega viral video. Online it began to rack up millions of social media views. I expected I would get some criticism, maybe even lots of criticism, because usually when you're outspoken about anything that goes viral online that happens. After all, witness my First Amendment and boobs brouhaha. I'd called every man in the Democrat Party a pussy. Heck, lots of left-wingers even refused to use the word "pussy," arguing it should be labeled the "p word" because it was laced with misogyny. (Whenever someone made that gender-based argument, I'd always respond, "Are you claiming calling someone a dickhead is a good thing?" Generally speaking, when you call someone a male or female genital, it isn't a positive thing.)

But something strange happened this time as my comments continued to go viral—even being played on-air on the opinion shows on CNN, MSNBC, and Fox News—almost everyone agreed with me.

And the younger the people were, the more they agreed with me.

The reaction to my comments at the University of Chicago event convinced me even more that young men, sports fans, and Trump had saved America. And it led to my decision to write this book. There are many things that I've written in this book that I believe are indisputably true and should be considered common sense to everyone. But, sadly, I'm not sure anyone else in the country would write what I have. In other words, if I didn't write it, this story wouldn't be told.

In many ways, I believe this book completes a trilogy. In *Republicans Buy Sneakers Too*, I laid out why the embrace of woke sports was divisive for America and the sports leagues. But that book, written in 2017 and published in 2018, was forward looking; the climb toward peak wokeness was still underway. It wouldn't be until the Lia Thomas NCAA swimming title on March 19, 2022, that we reached peak wokeness. (The moment of silence to protest the Florida education bill occurred the day before on March 18, 2022, which I would argue probably represented peak wokeness for ESPN.) The second book in this trilogy, *American Playbook*, laid out how Republicans could win in 2024, and today if you go read it, it stands as a virtual blueprint for the Trump 2024 campaign. I suspect at least some of his campaign advisers read it. And now this book completes the trilogy, chronicling our ultimate victory over the woke sports era.

I'm deeply proud of the impact OutKick has had in the country. If I hadn't founded OutKick back in 2011, there would have been no sports site to field the messages from Paula Scanlan and tell the story of the man on the University of Pennsylvania women's swimming team. There would have been no one out there to push back against the far-left-wing agenda in sports, no one to support—and later hire—Riley Gaines to help barnstorm the country and push back against the woke insanity. And, incredibly, there would have been no sports site to fight for sports to be played in 2020, when every other sports media company in America was filled with sportswriters screaming that playing sports was too dangerous in the Covid era. It's tempting to spike the football here, but I've learned that fighting for common sense and basic fairness in sports—and our culture—is always going to be a battle. I've learned that what feels like victory can be a loss and what feels like a loss can ultimately turn into a victory.

In May of 2021, I sold OutKick for enough money to make me a hundred millionaire. For a kid who grew up with two parents who never made more than $67,000 both working full-time for the state of Tennessee, it was a level of wealth I'd barely ever dreamed of. Early that morning, as the documents were signed, I told my wife we'd just paid for every kid and grandkid and great-grandkid we'd ever have to be able to go to any college in the country and pursue any educational dream they might ever have.

I slept for a couple of hours and then I got up and went back to work.

Everyone likes to daydream about what they would do if they won the lottery, if suddenly they had more money than they could ever spend in a lifetime. I've lived that dream. It's an incredible feeling. But do you know what's even better than winning the lottery? To wake up the next morning and keep doing exactly what you were doing already. Because if you win the lottery and then the next morning you wake up and keep doing exactly what you were already doing because you love it so much, well, let me tell you, that's true wealth.

The Atlantic editor who tried to cut my comments off in February said, "But Trump's like a grandpa!"

After my comments in response to her went viral, several young men who watched the exchange emailed me. They said they appreciated my comments and said that what Rosin missed was that many young men desperately look up to their grandpas. In particular, they see them as avatars of masculinity, stoic, tough, willing to bear the weight of the world on behalf of their families. And while I wrote this book and credited young men and sports fans for saving America, it's important to realize that the only reason we have an America to save in 2024 is because of the bravery of all our grandpas, the men who fought two world wars and ensured this country endured to the present day. Many young men see in older men a masculinity they aspire to one day embody. What Hannah Rosin saw as an insult—calling Trump a grandpa—many young men actually saw as the ultimate compliment.

For many of us, myself included, our grandpas are the toughest men we've ever known.

I'm named after Henry Clay Travis and Richard K. Fox, my paternal and maternal grandfathers. I've written quite a bit about Richard K. Fox, who played for the University of Tennessee in the 1930s and helped ensure I'd always be a University of Tennessee fan. I wrote much of his story in *Dixieland Delight*, my first book, published back in the summer of 2007. In fact, as I write this book in my home office, on the wall to my right is a framed program from the November 18, 1933, University of Tennessee football game against Vanderbilt. My grandfather is listed as 6'1" and 185 pounds, a twenty-year-old tackle. That was a big man back then. He told me he played football because they got unlimited food and a free dorm room. It was during the Depression, you see, and poor kids weren't that focused on games. They just wanted to have food to eat.

My paternal grandfather, Clay Travis, was twenty-eight years old back in 1933. As I said, he and my grandma never took a plane flight in their entire lives. In fact, the only places he really went for his entire life were between Goodlettsville, Tennessee, and Muhlenberg County, Kentucky, a place where all four of my great-grandparents on the Travis side are buried to this day, within a few feet of each other.

They are both the bravest and toughest men I have ever known. They, along with my own dad, are the reason I'm here today, and if I can be half the dad they all were, I know my own three boys will grow up to be outstanding fathers and husbands too. I never had to struggle with my own idea of what it meant to be a man because I was surrounded by strong men. Unfortunately today many young men aren't surrounded by strong men. It's why so many young men, I believe, gravitate toward Trump. They see in him a manhood that has been absent in many of their own lives.

I truly believe that every man reading this book has a tremendously important calling: We have to be better at raising true men than America has been in recent years. Young men, sports fans, and Trump may have saved the country in 2024.

But it's only one election.

If we truly want the legacy of this election win to endure, we have to use it as a foundation to return masculinity to the country, to make boy power real, to make manhood great again.

Personally, at forty-six years old, I think backward and forward now more than I used to, to where we all started and where we are all going. And I can't help but think that if in the space of two generations the Travis men can go from an eighth-grade education in Kentucky coal mine country to interviewing the president on Air

Force One, what can my own kids and grandkids accomplish in the next hundred years?

What can yours?

And what can we all accomplish together?

I'm more confident than I've ever been in this country and where we are all going together.

And somewhere, I truly believe this, all the badass grandpas and great-grandpas of America, including my own, Richard K. Fox and Henry Clay Travis, are looking down on us, hardworking as ever, proud that their grandsons are living their own versions of the American dream and confident that all our bests are still yet to come.

Thanks to sports fans, young men, and Trump, I can't wait to see where we are all headed. Trump has unlocked the voices of young men and sports fans, and I don't think either group will be silent in the years to come. So long as that remains true, the legacy of 2024 will be the conclusion of the woke era, the beginning of a return to common sense. Heck, maybe something truly crazy and revolutionary might even end up happening—men might even go back to playing sports against men instead of women.

ABOUT THE AUTHOR

Clay Travis is the founder of OutKick, the most influential sports media site on the internet, and the cohost of the *Clay Travis and Buck Sexton Show,* one of the nation's largest radio shows. He is the author of five books, including *Dixieland Delight, On Rocky Top, Republicans Buy Sneakers Too, American Playbook,* and *Balls.* A daily guest and commentator on Fox News, he has interviewed Donald Trump more than ten times, more than almost anyone in the country, including, most recently, live inside the stadium at the Georgia-Alabama game and on Air Force One en route to the NCAA wrestling tournament.

Also by Clay Travis

Dixieland Delight: A Football Season on the Road in
the Southeastern Conference

On Rocky Top: A Front-Row Seat to the End of an Era

Republicans Buy Sneakers Too: How the Left Is
Ruining Sports with Politics

American Playbook: A Guide to Winning Back the
Country from the Democrats